MW01671336

Payroll Auditing

A GUIDE FOR MULTIEMPLOYER PLANS

Lawrence R. Beebe
and Philip Vivirito

Payroll Auditing

A GUIDE FOR MULTIEMPLOYER PLANS

Lawrence R. Beebe
and Philip Vivirito

International Foundation
EDUCATION – BENEFITS • COMPENSATION
Accomplish More.

The opinions expressed in this book are those of the authors. The International Foundation of Employee Benefit Plans disclaims responsibility for views expressed and statements made in books published by the Foundation.

Edited by Judith A. Sankey, CEBS

Copies of this book may be obtained from:
Publications Department
International Foundation of Employee Benefit Plans
18700 West Bluemound Road
Brookfield, WI 53045

Payment must accompany order.

Call (888) 334-3327, option 4, for price information or see www.ifebp.org/bookstore.

Published in 2008 by the International Foundation of Employee Benefit Plans, Inc.

Library of Congress Control Number: 2008922921
ISBN 978-0-89154-643-6
Printed in the United States of America

1M-408

DEDICATION

We dedicate this book to Thomas E. Seay (1948-1997). Tom was an enthusiastic supporter of his accounting firm, Bond Beebe, and of the International Foundation of Employee Benefit Plans. Tom loved payroll auditing. In many ways, this book is his story.

Table of Contents

About the Authors

Mr. Beebe is a partner with the accounting firm of Bond Beebe, which is based in the Washington, D.C. metropolitan area. He was partner in charge of the firm's audit department for over 20 years and has served for many years as trustee and administrator of the firm's retirement plan. Mr. Beebe's accounting and auditing practice includes over 30 years of experience specializing in labor and employee benefit plans. He performs specialized work in the areas of forensic and operational auditing and often is called to testify as an expert witness in matters relating to those areas. Mr. Beebe has been a frequent instructor at the University of Maryland, professional associations throughout the United States, AICPA and the International Foundation. He has published a number of articles based on his teaching, and he assists in the annual revisions to the AICPA's Audits of Employee Benefit Plans and the AICPA's Employee Benefit Audit Risk Alert. Mr. Beebe is currently an Advisory Director to the International Foundation. He previously served on the Accountants Committee. Mr. Beebe also served on the AICPA Employee Benefit Expert Panel.

Mr. Vivirito is the director of payroll and compliance auditing for Bond Beebe. He has served in this position since joining Bond Beebe over five years ago. Prior to this time he spent 18 years as a field auditor, manager and department head for several offices. Mr. Vivirito has set up and coordinated payroll audit programs for various multiemployer funds. His experience ranges from payroll audits in the service industry, to building trades and 401(k) plans, and he has developed audit programs and reports to meet the unique needs of each type of fund. Mr. Vivirito has been a frequent speaker at conferences on the topic of payroll audits, and this book is his first major publication.

Chapter 1

Introduction

The purpose of this book is to aid those persons in a multiemployer employee benefit plan who are responsible for and who perform payroll audits. To date, there has been little guidance in this area. Included are the procedures and methodologies of performing an audit, as well as what are judged "best practices" in payroll auditing, recognizing that these practices differ based on factors such as the plan operations and the industry in which the employer operates. Tips for trustees and payroll auditors are offered where appropriate, and stories told by payroll auditors to illustrate the points under discussion are included.

A *payroll audit,* as the term is used in this book, is an audit of the records of a contributing employer in a multiemployer plan to determine if that employer has made the contributions required by the collective bargaining agreement (CBA) to the participating plan or plans. The primary purpose of the audit is to determine whether the contributing employer has fulfilled its responsibility to report all hours or wages required to be reported. The payroll audit is also utilized to determine any deficiencies or delinquencies that are due to the plan by the employer's failure to report all hours or wages for which contributions are required.

Trustees help fulfill their fiduciary duties by having payroll audits performed. In auditing the plan's financial statements, the external certified public accountant (CPA) utilizes payroll audits to gain assurance that all employer contributions that should have been remitted have been remitted.

Payroll Auditing vs. Compliance Auditing

Many plans now refer to the audits of contributing employers as *compliance audits,* rather than *payroll audits.* Why? The two reasons often cited are discussed below.

Payroll audit implies that the auditor will restrict himself or herself to payroll records. However, to be thorough, the audit effort must enable the auditor to review the employer's cash receipts, disbursement records and general ledger, and might even be extended to the employer's financial statements and income tax returns. In order for the auditor to judge whether the remittance reports are an accurate representation of the hours worked or paid to employees covered by the CBA, access to more than payroll records is essential. The trustees of the plans should draft the agreement and declaration of trust (or other document that permits auditor access) in such a way that the auditor can gain access to the records needed to complete a thorough examination.

Tips for Trustees

The agreement and declaration of trust should be as inclusive as possible in stating the records that the contributing employer should produce for the payroll auditor. Records that should be required include:

- Payroll records including details on hours worked and paid (weekly or monthly)
- Individual employees' earnings records (quarterly or yearly)
- Employer's federal Form 941 Quarterly Payroll Tax Returns and annual earnings reports: Forms W-2, W-3, 1099 and 1096
- Employer copies of monthly remittance reports to all fringe benefit funds to which the employer contributes
- Cash disbursement records
- All pertinent personnel information, such as a hire and termination list
- General ledger
- Records of payments made for leased employees
- Corporate or personal income tax returns.

A second reason for using the term *compliance audit,* instead of *payroll audit,* is that employers seem to be less offended by it. A payroll audit has a connotation similar to that of an Internal Revenue Service (IRS) audit. Compliance, on the other hand, suggests adherence to the set of rules that governs the plan. Is this just smoke and mirrors? Perhaps. In the future, the term *compliance audit* may replace the term *payroll audit.* However, until that happens, these audits will continue to be called payroll audits in this book.

Reasons for Conducting Payroll Audits

Section 405 of the Employee Retirement Income Security Act (ERISA) states that a trustee will not be liable for an act or omission if the trustee acted prudently and in the interest of participants and beneficiaries.[1] Why should trustees conduct payroll audits as part of their fiduciary responsibility?

Trustees have the responsibility to collect delinquent contributions.[2] This principle was set forth in the case of *Central States Pension Fund v. Central Transport, Inc.,*

The Quintessential Payroll Auditor

Tom Seay, who worked at Bond Beebe from 1970 until his untimely death in 1997, was the quintessential payroll auditor. He didn't think anyone was a better payroll auditor than he was, and he was probably right. Long after he became a partner at Bond Beebe and didn't have to do field work any longer, Tom would take his annual two-to-three-week trip across the United States to do payroll audits. Off he would go in his little red sports car, often accompanied by his faithful companion, Charlie Wendal. They would crisscross the United States doing payroll audits as they went along. Tom enjoyed meeting new people and he enjoyed the challenge of getting to the heart of an employer's payroll records in the few hours devoted to each job. Tom loved doing payroll audits, and he loved reciting the stories of what he found on his sojourns. Many of the payroll auditor's stories in this book are Tom Seay stories. Payroll auditors love to tell stories. We will tell a number of these stories in this book.

A Payroll Auditor's Story

"When performing a payroll audit, I often make a judgment call in deciding how much time to spend looking at an employer's cash disbursement records. At a minimum, I see whether any subcontracting payments are being made to individuals that might be for work covered by the CBA. If I find a great number of errors in the payroll records, I try to spend additional time examining cash disbursements. The time spent examining these records is often worth the effort."

—*Tom Seay*

472 U.S. 559 (1985). The court rejected the argument that the responsibility for collecting delinquencies was that of the union, the Department of Labor or the beneficiaries. ERISA has given this responsibility to the trustees, and if the trustees don't fulfill this responsibility in a prudent manner, they can be held personally liable.

To fulfill the responsibility trustees have for delinquent contributions, he or she should insist that the trust fund have a detailed written collection policy for the administrative staff to follow. A prudently written collection policy calls for a methodology of auditing the contributions made by contributing employers. The form and content of the payroll audit program should be a part of the document's written collection policy. The collection policy is further described in Chapter 15. An example of a written collection policy can be found in Appendix A.

Another reason for conducting payroll audits has to do with the plan's audited financial statements. The independent auditors of employee benefit plans must follow certain requirements set down by the accounting profession. Primary among these requirements is that the audit must be conducted in accordance with generally accepted auditing standards (GAAS). An auditor who deviates from GAAS in conducting an audit is subject to civil and criminal liability as well as potential loss of license and/or other sanctions by the American Institute of Certified Public Accountants (AICPA).

One of the ten GAAS requires the independent auditor to gather sufficient evidential matter to support the opinion rendered by the CPA on the plan's financial statements. As part of gathering this evidential matter, the auditor must verify the income of the plan, including employer contributions. In a multiemployer plan audit it is difficult, if not impossible, to gather enough information regarding the completeness of employer contributions without doing payroll audits.

AICPA has published an audit guide titled *Audits of Employee Benefit Plans.* Audit guides are interpretations of GAAS and must be adhered to by CPAs. The audit guide states that in audits of multiemployer plans, the auditor should compare the employer's contribution reports with information shown in the participant's payroll records to gain information about participant data. The guide does not use the term *payroll audit,* but the requirement is clear. The guide suggests several alternatives to payroll audits, but each of these alternatives has its own complications and risks.

What happens if the auditor cannot gather the necessary information about participant data? In such a circumstance, the auditor will not be able to give an unqualified opinion. A qualified opinion, or disclaimer of opinion, must be given instead because the scope of the auditor's work was not sufficient. As explained in the following paragraph, the failure to have an unqualified opinion can have disastrous consequences for a plan.

If a plan has more than 100 participants, the Department of Labor (DOL) and the Internal Revenue Service (IRS) require that an independent auditor's report be attached to the plan's financial statements, which accompany the federal Form 5500. DOL will not accept an auditor's report that has been qualified because of the failure by the trustees to have a payroll audit program. When the filing is rejected because of a qualified opinion, DOL treats the filing as if it were a nonfiling. DOL can assess penalties of up to $1,100 per day against plan administrators who fail to file timely and complete reports.[3]

Other factors requiring the imposition of a payroll audit program include:

1. Ideally, all employers pay their contributions to employee trust funds because they are genuinely concerned about the welfare of their workers. For many employers, this is true. For others, the only factor that may keep them honest is the fear that they will be caught and penalized if they don't pay when required. A payroll audit program puts the less-than-honorable employer on notice that the trustees are serious about collecting deficiencies. If Employer X down the street is audited and penalized for nonreporting, then Employer Y may pay what is owed to avoid the same penalties. Payroll auditing works in a manner similar to preventive medicine.
2. Another reason to conduct payroll audits is to deal with the suspicion that an employer is not fulfilling the terms of the CBA. Complaints may be received when annual statements are sent to participants. Local union officials may complain that the employer is not properly reporting all employees working in job classifications covered by the CBA. The payroll audit should find these unreported employees. However, if the employer hides or disguises payments to such employees in a manner such as paying employees in cash, the payroll audit may not be successful in discovering the problem.
3. An employer may go nonunion or not renew the CBA. In addition to the withdrawal liability that may be created by such action, the plan should conduct a final payroll audit to determine whether the employer properly remitted up until the date of termination.
4. New employers often present a problem. Many funds have a policy of auditing new employers after six or nine months of reporting. As part of the audit process, the employer can be trained how to report properly.
5. When an employer experiences financial difficulty, payment of the employees' fringe benefits slows or often stops completely. Most plans have a mechanism to police such delinquencies. If an employer fails to cooperate with the ensuing collection enforcement action, the plan will refer the matter to legal counsel. Legal counsel often requests a payroll audit as part of the enforcement action.
6. Employers that cease to be covered by a CBA also present a problem. Employers may stop their contributions before the CBA expires. A payroll audit on terminating employers ensures that remittances are sent through the termination date of the CBA.

Delinquencies vs. Deficiencies

A payroll audit is designed primarily to identify deficiencies in amounts remitted by contributing employers. The employer has submitted a remittance report detailing hours worked or wages paid to employees covered by the CBA. The audit then identifies an underpayment or overpayment to the plan due to an intentional or unintentional error in reporting hours worked or wages paid. If the amount is an underpayment, it is referred to as a *deficiency.* A deficiency is distinguished from a delinquency. A *delinquency* occurs when the employer has not submitted and remitted for required remittance reports. The payroll audit can also encompass the period of the delinquency to ensure that the reporting by the employer is correct.

A Payroll Auditor's Story

"On one payroll audit I found substantial deficiencies. As I explained this to the employer, his reply was, 'If you think I'm bad, you ought to see how some of my competitors cheat.' I asked him to provide the names of the 'cheating' competitors. He did. When we performed payroll audits on the competitors, we found large deficiencies in each of them."

—Larry Beebe

Endnotes

1. Thomas E. Funk, "Delegation of Responsibility," *Trustees Handbook,* Fourth Edition, International Foundation of Employee Benefit Plans.

2. Ira R. Mitzner, "The Art of Collection," *Trustees Handbook,* Fourth Edition, International Foundation of Employee Benefit Plans.

3. ERISA Section 502(c)(2).

Chapter 2

Performing the Payroll Audit

Now that the trustees have decided that payroll audits should be conducted on contributing employers, a key question is: Who should perform the payroll audits? Plan personnel can either perform the audits internally, or third parties external to the plan can perform them. What are the considerations as to whether the audits should be performed by internal or external auditors?

Internal Payroll Audit Program

The decision to operate a payroll audit program internally is not a decision to be taken lightly by the trustees. The plan administrator may do an excellent job in administering the plan in all other respects, but still may fail to operate an effective payroll audit program. Why? Because administration of such a program often takes more time and attention than an administrator can give.

The first decision to make is who will administer the payroll audit program. If the administrator does not have the time and/or the background to manage the payroll audit program, then someone else should do it. That person will be called the payroll audit manager.

The ideal payroll audit manager would have a degree in accounting and at least some experience in payroll auditing. In lieu of the degree, the payroll audit manager should have years of experience in the operation of payroll audit programs. Other attributes of the payroll audit manager should include:

- **Analytical skills.** The payroll audit program should be established on a logical and rational basis to collect maximum deficiencies and delinquencies with a minimum of cost.
- **Organizational skills.** The payroll audit program must be properly scheduled, the audits conducted as scheduled and the reports to the trustees prepared and delivered on a timely basis.
- **People skills.** The auditors performing the payroll audits must be properly trained, supervised and managed.
- **Efficiency.** A payroll audit manager must be efficient in managing people and costs.

Advantages

A properly managed internal payroll audit program has advantages compared to an external payroll audit program. These advantages include:

- **Cost.** If managed properly, an internal payroll audit program should be less costly than an external payroll audit program. An external payroll audit program has a profit factor built into the amount billed to the client. Assuming that the payroll audit program is being managed internally at its maximum cost efficiency, the internally managed payroll audit program should be less expensive.

- **Control of the audit steps.** The trustees, the plan administrator and/or the payroll audit manager may insist that certain procedures be performed in every payroll audit. The program detailing these required steps will be completed by the auditor and reviewed by the payroll audit manager. As part of the review process, the payroll audit manager can ensure that all required audit steps were performed.
- **Easier quality measurement.** If the trustees hire an external auditor to perform payroll audits, the only document they receive is the audit report itself. With only the report it is difficult, if not impossible, to measure the quality of the individual audit. With an internal audit program, the payroll audit manager reviews the working paper files for each individual audit and can come to a decision regarding the quality of that audit.
- **Control of the audit program.** If external payroll auditors are hired, the trustees may not be their most important client. The trustees may not get audit reports when they want them. Trustees also have no control over the quality of the auditors and the quality of the work they are performing. Performing payroll audits internally means the trustees control the quality and timeliness of the audits.
- **Use of payroll auditors to perform other plan functions.** When payroll audits are done internally, they can be scheduled to suit the trustees' schedule. If trustees have times when payroll auditors could be best used to perform other plan functions, the trustees don't have to schedule payroll audits for those times. This might mean savings in personnel costs for the plan.
- **Gathering additional information during the payroll audits.** Periodically, the plan may need to gather certain information about its contributing employers that can be used to streamline operations. Examples could be information about the employer's payroll system, computer systems or cash disbursement systems. Internal auditors conducting payroll audits could efficiently gather information of this type.
- **Educating the employers that are audited.** Internal payroll auditors can educate the employer concerning reporting requirements and inform the employer regarding plan operations. This can only be done effectively by using an internal audit staff.

Disadvantages

The disadvantages of the internal payroll audit program are:

- **Training.** A person educated in accounting and auditing needs specialized training to become an efficient payroll auditor. This should include training in how unions operate; the workings of the collective bargaining agreement (CBA) and various plan documents; and the peculiarities of payroll auditing compared to other types of auditing. If trustees hire their own auditors internally, this training becomes the trustees' problem. If trustees hire external auditors, then it becomes the auditors' problem.

- **Turnover.** Those who are hired as payroll auditors typically remain on the job for no more than one or two years. The work is very repetitive and is done under high-stress conditions. The auditor has to travel to and find the employer. The auditor is made to feel as welcome as an IRS auditor and has to confront the employer with the deficiencies found as a result of the audit. All of this leads to burnout and turnover. If trustees hire the auditor, it is the trustees' problem. If trustees hire external auditors, it is the auditors' problem.
- **Dead-end career path.** An employee benefit plan is seldom able to offer the internal payroll auditor a path for career advancement. This means that trustees don't keep their best auditors very long because these auditors don't see a future with the plan.

External Payroll Audit Program

The plan may decide that it does not want to operate its own internal payroll audit program, but would rather contract externally for the service. The plan must decide which of three types of entities to use for the payroll audit program:

1. **The same CPA firm that does the annual audit of the plan's financial statements.** The primary advantage to this arrangement is that the CPA firm doing the plan's annual audit should have an excellent understanding of how the plan operates and should know and understand the plan, the agreement and declaration of trust, the collective bargaining agreement and other documents under which the plan operates. Often the CPA firm has a different individual in charge of its payroll audit department than the partner in charge of the audit engagement. The trustees and plan administrator should ensure that the payroll audit program offered by its CPA firm meets its needs and is price competitive compared to alternatives offered by other firms.
2. **A CPA firm other than the CPA firm auditing the plan's financial statements.** The trustees may decide to utilize a different CPA firm to do its payroll audits. This allows the trustees to maintain a relationship with two different CPA firms and utilize the advantages that each has to offer. The same criteria should be used to judge the CPA firm doing the payroll audits as were used in the selection process for the CPA firm doing the audit of financial statements.
3. **An external firm, not holding itself out as a CPA firm, that specializes in payroll audits.** The advantage in hiring such a firm may be that it offers hourly rates for its services that may be less than a CPA firm. A non-CPA firm will not be subject to the standards of a CPA firm; therefore, the trustees must ensure that such a firm has its own standards, to ensure a quality payroll audit program for the plan.

Advantages

The advantages of an external payroll audit program are:

- **Cost sharing.** Firms hired to do external audit programs often have many clients. External auditors can arrange to do a payroll audit of a given employer where all plans covering a given trade and/or the plans for different unions can be audited at the same time. This allows the audit cost to be shared by the plans included in the audit. This same technique could be used by an internally directed audit program, but would be much more difficult to arrange and to manage.

- **Training and turnover.** External payroll auditing firms have multiple clients, and thus they normally have more than one payroll auditor. The more payroll auditors a firm has, the easier it is to train those employees. One person leaving is not as severe a problem when the firm has many payroll auditors.
- **Specialists.** The more auditors an external firm has, the more likely it is to have specialists. Some auditors are quick; others are more methodical. Some auditors specialize in identifying fraud and other irregularities, and others are best at routine audits. The external firm specializing in payroll audits may use these specialists effectively in operating its payroll audit programs.
- **Bonuses and other incentives.** An external firm specializing in payroll audits may offer bonus payments conditional on the auditor remaining on the job for a certain length of time and meeting certain performance standards. Payroll auditors may be offered the chance to be promoted to the financial audit department after satisfactory completion of a specialized length of service. These incentives may not be able to be offered by internal payroll audit programs.

Disadvantages

The disadvantages of an external audit program are:

- **Control of the audit program.** If the payroll audit program is external the trustees give up an element of control over the overall program. The trustees can mitigate this loss of control by establishing parameters that the eternal auditors must follow and by closely monitoring the overall program.
- **Cost.** An external audit program normally costs more because of the profit realized by the external auditors. This is based on the assumption, however, that the internal audit program will be efficiently managed.

Internal vs. External Auditors— It's Trustees' Choice

Now that internal and external payroll audit programs have been compared, which should be chosen for the plan? The decision must be made by each plan, taking into account its differences and similarities to other plans. The choice made is not important. What is important is that the plan constantly monitors the payroll audit program at the trustee level and makes decisions concerning the future direction of the program based on the best interests of the plan.

Choosing an External Audit Program

Once trustees choose to contract with a firm to do payroll audits for the plan, there are two additional steps to perform:

1. **Engagement letter.** The engagement letter should set forth the arrangements for the payroll audits that are to be performed. The auditor normally

sends the letter to the plan. The plan signs this letter and returns it to the auditor. An example of an engagement letter is contained in Appendix B. The engagement letter should normally document the arrangements between the two parties.

2. **The auditor's report.** The auditor's report, described fully in Chapter 15, states that certain agreed-upon procedures have been performed in the payroll audit. These procedures have been agreed to by the trustees and the auditor. These procedures are in the payroll audit program utilized by the auditor, which is described in Chapter 5. The trustees should understand the procedures that the auditors will utilize and measure the sufficiency of the procedures.

Chapter 3

Selecting the Employers to Be Audited

Which employers should be audited? Trustees may have been told that the Department of Labor (DOL) requires that every employer be audited in a three-year (or some other length) cycle. This is not true. DOL mandates only that trustees pursue delinquent or deficient employer contributions. How often the employer is audited is a decision for the trustees to make. The appropriate frequency of payroll auditing for one plan may be entirely different than for another plan.

Random Audits

To ensure that all contributing employers have a possibility of being audited, every year the plan should perform some or most of its audits on a random basis. Auditing every employer every three years may not be cost-efficient and would not be possible in a national plan containing thousands of employers.

Frequency Depends on Deficiencies Identified

The number of payroll audits performed annually should be constantly reviewed. A plan may institute a payroll audit program in which it decides to audit each employer in a three-year cycle. As this program proceeds, the plan may discover that most of its employers are reporting accurately, and therefore, a four- or six-year cycle might be more appropriate. The plan will also find, over time, that certain employers always report accurately and can therefore be audited less frequently; and that other employers are constantly delinquent or deficient in their reporting and should be audited more frequently.

A Payroll Auditor's Story

"I performed a payroll audit on a large employer and found significant deficiencies. The employer's controller admitted to me that the company did not timely file state income tax returns when the company worked in a given state, but instead waited for the state to 'catch up' with it. I concluded that the company was very casual regarding its obligations and therefore recommended to the plan that the employer be audited often. Every time the employer was audited subsequently, significant deficiencies were found."

—*Larry Beebe*

Tips for Trustees

At least annually, the trustees should have the administrator of the fund present statistics that compare the costs of the payroll audit program with the deficiencies identified and collected. If the cost of audits is increasing as a percentage of delinquencies identified, then it may be appropriate to cut down on the number of audits in the next year. Conversely, if deficiencies are increasing compared to audit cost, then more audits should be performed in the next year.

Problem Employers

Performing random audits annually is essential. An efficient and effective payroll audit program will aggressively pursue payroll audits of employers whose reporting practices are suspect for accuracy and completeness.

These problem employers should be audited frequently:

- Delinquent employers. The plan should target employers that are not reporting on a timely basis. The plan should have a policy that any employer known to be delinquent for a specified number of months (normally somewhere between three and six months) should be audited immediately. An employer that is constantly late in reporting should also be audited more frequently than an employer who is never late.
- Plan participants complain that they are denied benefits they have earned. If one or more participants is vocal when benefits are denied, stating that they have earned the necessary hours or units for benefits, then the circumstances should be investigated. This also can occur when participants are sent annual statements showing reported wages or hours. Participants are often asked to produce pay stubs or other documentation proving the necessary hours or units were worked. As part of this investigation, a payroll audit is often appropriate.
- Business agents report that not all covered employees are being reported or that not all hours are being reported by an employer.
- An employer has a nonunion company, which is suspected of being an alter ego for his union company. This situation is fully described in Chapter 14. Often a payroll audit can help determine whether an alter ego situation exists and whether deficiencies result from this situation.
- The employer is suspected of not reporting subcontractors or leased employers. The CBA requires reporting all hours for all individuals covered by the CBA. Just because an employer-employee relationship does not exist, this does not excuse reporting on the part of the employer.
- The remittance reports show patterns that suggest underreporting. The plan administrator should be directed by the trustees to look for underreporting. Examples would be remittance reports that never show overtime hours (if the plan requires remitting for all hours paid), or the consistent reporting of the minimum hours in a reporting period.

- The employer reports an employee or employees for several months; then the names disappear from the remittance report only to reappear again later. If this pattern persists, it is a sign of an employer shifting employees between a union company and a nonunion company. This situation should be investigated by having a payroll audit performed.
- Withdrawal liability. When an employer withdraws from the plan, a payroll audit should be performed through the date of withdrawal. The audit results can be used in the calculation of withdrawal liability (if any) for the employer.
- New employer. A new employer may not understand the reporting requirements of the plan. A payroll audit conducted within a year of the employer signing the CBA often helps to ensure that the employer is reporting properly to the plan. An audit may also be worthwhile within a year after a new person begins preparing and submitting remittance reports for the employer for the same reason. If ownership of the employer changes, a payroll audit within a reasonable time would also be appropriate.

TIPS FOR TRUSTEES

Don't assume that a complaint by one employee is an isolated instance. It may be the tip of the iceberg. In one instance an employee reported that he had been shorted 40 hours out of 1,800 reported. A payroll audit was performed and the employer was found not to have reported one week's hours for all employees. A deficiency of $20,000 was identified and collected as a result of this one complaint.

Consideration of Location

Location of the employer payroll records may be an important consideration in deciding how often to audit employers. If the plan covers a very small geographic area, then travel to the employers to conduct audits is not of any concern. However, if the geographic area covered by the plan is large, then travel costs must be considered. Employers in proximity to one another should be audited at the same time. Auditors should be instructed to conserve travel costs in auditing out-of-town employers. This subject is fully discussed in Chapter 9.

Controlling the Quality of Payroll Audits

Payroll audits can be inefficiently performed and thus be costly to the plan, or they can be done efficiently and promptly. Key elements in ensuring this quality are engagement management, the quality of the auditor, efficiency and proper payroll audit administration.

Engagement Management

Engagement management includes scheduling, performance of audit field work, producing and issuing the report, and dealing with problems.

Scheduling

Scheduling the audit with the employer seems like a simple process. Just pick up the telephone and tell the employer when the auditor will be there. What could be easier? Unfortunately it doesn't usually work that way.

The first step is to have the plan send a letter to the employer stating that it has been selected for a payroll audit and notifying it that the auditor (or his or her representative) will be calling to schedule the audit. An example of an audit notification letter is shown in Appendix C.

Tips for Trustees

You should consider sending the audit notification letter by certified mail with return receipt requested. This helps ensure that the letter was received and will be acknowledged.

Then a phone call should be made to the employer. The caller should either be the auditor or an administrative person who has been trained to make these phone calls. The person making the call should note the details of every phone call made to the employer. This record may prove useful in those rare situations where litigation is necessary as part of the payroll audit process.

The auditor's representative should ask to speak to the person at the employer who can schedule the payroll audit. That person usually works in the accounting department, but in some instances may be the employer itself. The auditor's representative should ask the employer's representative if the letter notifying the employer of the payroll audit was received. If the employer representative states that the letter was not received, then a copy should be faxed immediately.

The goal of the auditor's representative is to schedule the payroll audit at a date and time that is convenient to the payroll auditor. The auditor's representative might say, "We will be in your area on Tuesday, April 20, and would like the audit to start at 8:00 a.m. that morning."

Tips for Trustees

1. Avoid letting the employer set the start time. Employers will inevitably set 10:00 a.m. or 2:00 p.m., and this does not leave the auditor enough time to do a proper audit.
2. Have back-up times and dates available if the employer cannot do the audit when you want to do it.

The auditor's representative should be aware that a small number of employers will not agree to schedule the payroll audit. These employers may not return phone calls or may offer numerous excuses as to why the audit cannot be scheduled. The representative should be trained to recognize these tactics and should notify the plan's collection attorney when the employer is being unreasonable in scheduling the payroll audit.

The auditor's representative should ask certain questions to gather information that will streamline the audit process for the payroll auditor. These questions may be in the form of a questionnaire.

The questionnaire should gather the following information from the employer:

1. What are the total number of employees on the payroll and how many are covered by the CBA?
2. Is the payroll prepared in-house or by a payroll provider?
3. If prepared by an outside contractor, is that contractor either ADP or Paychex?
4. Is the payroll organized by department and, if so, which departments are covered by the CBA?
5. Are all hours reported, or is there a probationary period before reporting begins?
6. Are vacation and holiday hours reported?
7. Has the same person prepared remittance reports for the entire period of the payroll audit?
8. Does the employer hire employees from a temporary employment agency to perform work covered by the CBA?
9. Does the employer use subcontractors to perform work covered by the CBA and, if so, were Form 1099s issued?

Tips for Trustees

If payroll is prepared by either ADP or Paychex, ask the employer for the quarterly payroll by employee. Use of this quarterly listing should save considerable time in the audit.

Performance of Audit Field Work

The key to performance in a payroll audit is to be well organized. When the auditor arrives at the employer, he or she should quickly establish who at the organization will answer questions and provide information during field work. Immediately the auditor should determine that all records requested are available and have been provided.

The goal in auditing the records is to perform the work in the time allotted for the

A Payroll Auditor's Story

"I use a pre-audit questionnaire. In this case, the employer filled out the answers to the questions and faxed the questionnaire. One question asked whether there was a probationary period before contributions began. The employer said that 720 hours had to be worked before a new hire was reported. The rules of the plan stated that new hires were to be reported immediately. When the audit started, I asked for a list of new hires and quickly identified a deficiency of several thousand dollars."

—Phil Vivirito

audit. The auditor should avoid, if at all possible, going back to the employer for a second day when few or no deficiencies are found the first day. If the auditor does not find deficiencies the first day, then it is unlikely that deficiencies will be found the second day.

Providing and Issuing the Report

The key to producing an effective and efficient payroll audit report is timeliness. If the auditor has time in the field at the conclusion of the audit, the report should be started as soon as evidence gathering has concluded. On out-of-town engagements, the auditor can get a start on the report by doing work in the hotel at night. The point is to work on the report while the work is fresh in the auditor's mind. Time for drafting the report should be scheduled just as the audit field work should be scheduled. If an audit report takes weeks or months to prepare, the results will not be satisfactory to either the auditor or the benefit plan.

Another factor in preparing a satisfactory payroll audit report is to use terminology that the employer and the plan understand. Plans often have unique wording to refer to documents and/or processes within the plan. If the auditor uses terminology familiar to the plan, there is a better chance that the report will be accepted by all parties as originally written.

Dealing With Problems

The auditor must have a specific person to contact at the employer. This person should provide all necessary information to the auditor and should make decisions so the audit can proceed and be concluded in a timely manner. The auditor should also know the person to call at the plan who can make the decisions that allow the audit to progress. Often a problem arises in a payroll audit that the auditor does not resolve on a timely basis and the job is then delayed. The auditor also needs a person in his or her own organization who can solve problems as they arise. Knowing whom to contact to resolve the problem and determining to solve the problem earlier rather than later avoids unneeded delays in completion of a payroll audit.

Quality of the Auditor

Finding excellent payroll auditors is not an easy task. Some people are excellent internal auditors, and others function best as external auditors examining a company's financial statements. Unfortunately, just because someone is a good auditor does not make that person a good payroll auditor. Finding the right payroll auditor or auditors is such an important part of the entire process that both Chapter 6 and Chapter 7 of this book discuss the topic.

Efficiency of the Payroll Audit

Efficiency in performing the payroll audit is extremely important. The three elements of an efficient payroll audit are timeliness, cost and avoiding the unnecessary.

Unless the payroll audit is performed and delivered on a timely basis, it is of little use to anyone. A timely audit is one that is scheduled promptly, completed within a reasonable period of time, delivered to the plan administrator as scheduled, forwarded to the company that was audited without delay and quickly followed up on for collection if any amount due is shown on the audit.

No one wants to pay for an inefficiently performed payroll audit. Sending an auditor to a contributing employer's place of business is an expensive proposition at best, but the audit becomes even more expensive if the auditor isn't doing everything it can to maximize efficiency on the job. Every time the auditor has to pick up the job it costs more money. The most efficient payroll audit is one where the auditor does the field work in one visit to the employer and then is able to write the report from start to finish without coming back to it a second time.

Problems are inevitable in the payroll audit process. How the auditor and the payroll audit administrator handle those problems often dictates how efficient the audit is. Every attempt should be made to solve the problem, resolving all issues, as soon as it arises. The smart payroll auditor also anticipates problems and is prepared to deal with them as they arise.

TIPS FOR TRUSTEES

The trustees should rarely, if ever, be involved in the routine matters of the payroll audit program. Routine matters should be set up to be handled completely by the payroll audit administrator. The trustees should deal with payroll audits and collections only where the matter can't be resolved by the normal routine process.

Payroll Audit Administration

The payroll auditors may do their job as efficiently as possible. Even so, the payroll audit process may fail because it is not properly administered. In order to succeed, a payroll audit administrator must be properly educated and trained, must be decisive and must have the authority to do the job.

How can someone be trained and educated to supervise a payroll audit program? Certainly that person does not have to be a CPA, but he or she must know and understand how multiemployer plans operate. The administrator must have a working knowledge of CBAs and their provisions. The administrator must also have some knowledge of the law as it affects payroll audits and collections. Most often the administrator worked as a payroll auditor before advancing to the position of administrator. The administrator should also attend continuing education programs, such as the International Foundation of Employee Benefit Plans' Collection Procedures Institute, to keep up with the latest about payroll audits and collections.

A good payroll audit administrator must be decisive. If the administrator procrastinates in making decisions, the payroll audits become drawn out and costly. The payroll audit administrator must also be consistent in decision making.

The payroll audit administrator may be doing the best job possible, but the program still may fail if the administrator isn't given the authority to do the job. The administrator should have complete authority over the payroll auditors and should have authorization to deal with the contributing employers being audited over routine matters.

Chapter 5

Controlling Payroll Audit Costs

Once a payroll audit program is established, what can be done to the program to ensure that trustees are spending their payroll audit dollars wisely? What techniques have others learned that will save money in a payroll audit program?

The Audit Program

The audit program is a series of steps the auditor performs in the course of the job. Two examples of audit programs are shown in Appendixes D and E. Why are there two examples of payroll audit programs? There are many steps that can be performed in a payroll audit and no one approach is better than any other. Two different examples of payroll audit programs are provided so that trustees can decide what works best for them. It may be the program in Appendix D, or the one in Appendix E or a combination of the two, or it may be the trustees' own audit program.

There are two types of audit programs. One is very rigid. The auditor must perform every step in the audit program and should not deviate from the steps shown. The other audit program allows flexibility and audit judgment on the part of the auditor. Certain steps in the program will always be performed, and others will be performed based on the circumstances the auditor finds in auditing each employer.

Should payroll audits be performed using a rigid payroll audit program or a flexible audit program? If the auditor is inexperienced, a rigid program may be appropriate for the first few audits performed. Under normal circumstances, however, a flexible audit program is best suited to the performance of an efficient payroll audit. Every payroll audit is different. Some employers are large and some are small. Some employ only workers covered by the collective bargaining agreement (CBA) and some employ many trades. Some employers' payroll records are simple and others have complicated records. The rigid payroll audit program attempts to fit all circumstances. Performance of every step in an audit program designed to fit all circumstances results in inefficient payroll audits. If trustees adequately train their auditors, the trustees can be given flexibility in performing the audit.

Should the Entire Population Be Audited?

There are two schools of thought as to whether a 100% audit for all hours for all employees covered by the CBA should be done. Some say always do a 100% audit because even a ten- or 20-hour shortage could mean the difference between a person receiving or not receiving a pension.

Others feel, as do the authors, that a 100% audit violates the cost/benefit relationship. The cost of obtaining audit evidence should not outweigh the benefit obtained. Doing a 100% audit of the population, except in those instances where the population is very small, could take thousands of dollars of audit time. Can trustees justify a payroll audit that costs $20,000 if a deficiency of only $308 is found?

Judgmental vs. Statistical Sampling

Statistical sampling is used by an auditor who wants to project the sample results to a population. For example, the auditor might find 40 vacation hours unreported in a sample of 2,000 hours tested. If the population was 50,000 hours, then the auditor might state in the projection to the population that 1,000 vacation hours were unreported. The auditor sampled 1/25th of the population and multiplied the sample results by 25 to get the projected population variance.

The problem with the above approach is that no contributing employer will pay for a projected variance of 1,000 hours. The employer wants to know exactly who was shorted and how many hours each person was shorted. The plan administrator wants the same information.

Statistical sampling in a payroll audit sounds wonderful in theory, but it just does not work. The efficient payroll audit judgmentally samples the population, looking for deficiencies. When deficiencies are identified, the auditor expands the sample searching for the same type of deficiencies and finds the name of the employee for each deficiency identified.

Identifying Unreported Covered Employees

What specific steps should the payroll auditor perform in identifying and summarizing unreported hours for covered employees?

1. **Review wage rates.** Since wage rates are specified in the CBA, identifying all employees with the wage rates shown in the CBA is often the way to identify covered employees.
2. **Review employee classifications.** Often the classification in the payroll records and/or the personnel files identifies covered employees.
3. **Eliminate clerical employees and management.** Clerical employees and management are often paid by the week or by the month, whereas covered employees are often paid by the hour.
4. **Review remittance reports submitted to other trades.** This often eliminates those hourly wage employees who belong to other unions.

Test Several Frequently Reported Employees

Once the auditor has decided which employees should have been reported, he or she should compare actual hours to hours reported.

First, the payroll auditor should take one or two employees who are reported regularly and trace their hours for an entire calendar quarter or year, from the payroll records to the remittance reports. This is done so that the auditor can ensure that he or she understands the payroll system utilized by the employer. Once the auditor understands the system, the auditor should concentrate on identifying any errors that exist.

Concentrate on Errors

Once the auditor understands how the payroll system operates, he or she should start looking for the error types that are identified in Chapter 10. Once a reporting error is found, the auditor should test for potential errors of the same type to see if a pattern emerges. For example, if the auditor finds that vacation hours have not been reported on one employee, he or she should test payments of other vacation hours to see if they have been reported. If the auditor continues to find errors in vacation hours reported, he or she should test all vacation hours paid to determine the total deficiency for this type of reporting error.

The payroll auditor then tests for potential errors in each area where an error is likely to exist. Once the auditor is convinced that the employer is reporting correctly in each area tested, no additional testing is necessary in that area.

Avoid the Proof Mentality

Auditors love to prove the arithmetical accuracy of certain numbers in the financial statements. For example, a payroll auditor could prove that the gross wages for all employees equal total wages paid on the annual W-3 filed with the federal government. Most often this proof is a waste of time and should be avoided. A better test is to review the W-2s to ensure that the auditor has been keeping payroll records for all employees.

The only time that an auditor should prove total payroll is when he or she is convinced that the payroll records do not accurately reflect the entire payroll paid by the employer. Proving payroll does little to help the payroll auditor find deficiencies.

Tips for Trustees

Many payroll providers prepare W-2s, W-3s and payroll reconciliations as part of the services they provide to an employer. There is no need for the auditor to duplicate the work already performed by the provider.

Communicating With the Employer

Once the auditor has identified all the deficiencies during field work, should the auditor communicate these findings to the employer before returning to the office to

A Payroll Auditor's Story

"An employer's bookkeeper provided me with individual earnings records and quarterly payroll tax returns for the year. Gross wages for one of the quarters were over $750,000. I had only been given ten individual earnings records at an average wage rate of $13 per hour. I was convinced I did not have the entire payroll. After questioning the bookkeeper frequently, I was told that I had not been given the payroll records for the 'other company.' When the payroll records for the 'other company' were finally produced, I found a significant deficiency."

—Phil Vivirito

write the report? Some plans require the auditor to have an exit interview, and others don't want it to take place.

Those plans that favor the exit interview claim that it saves time and money. The employer is shown the deficiencies found and is given the opportunity to present additional information and/or evidence as to why the deficiency or deficiencies identified are not accurate. Once the auditor leaves the field, he or she normally has agreement from the employer acknowledging that the deficiencies noted are accurate.

Other plans don't want an exit interview because the auditor isn't finished with the audit. The auditor has to check plan and/or union records to determine if certain individuals are reportable. This is often true in the building trades or other unions where employees work sporadically or move frequently from employer to employer. Having an exit interview under this set of circumstances does not make sense because the audit is not complete.

Producing the Report Quickly

Once the audit field work has been completed, time should be scheduled in the office for the auditor to complete his or her report on a timely basis. If possible, the audit report should be completed, from start to finish, in one work session. The more often the auditor picks up and puts down the audit, the longer it takes to do the job. If report writing takes place too long after the completion of field work, the auditor forgets what was done and the report writing takes longer. Every payroll auditor should have a sign over his or her desk that says, "Complete the payroll audit on a timely basis. Get it out the door."

Giving the Auditor Flexibility

The advantages of giving the auditor flexibility in completing the audit program have already been cited. One of these advantages is that the auditor doesn't have to spend valuable time, which could better be spent in writing the audit report, in documenting audit procedures that were not necessary to perform.

Coordination With the Business Agent or Local Union

Often the business agent or some other local union official will have valuable information that the auditor can use in the audit. For example, the business agent might say, "I know that XYZ Company is not reporting overtime hours." The payroll auditor can immediately concentrate on the identified errors, saving audit time.

There may be legitimate reasons why the plan does not want the payroll auditor to contact anyone from the local union before performing an audit. The payroll auditor should take guidance from the plan administrator in this area.

Sharing Costs

Often the CBA covers more than one plan. If all plans covered by the same agreement agree to share audit costs, the payroll audit can be done to cover all plans. Audit costs are then normally prorated based on the contribution rate for each plan. For example, if total contributions for all plans covered by the payroll audits are $6 per hour and the pension plan is $1.50 per hour, then the pension plan would pay for 25% of the cost of auditing for all the plans. This sharing of audit costs can be done regardless of whether all plans are local, or whether one or more plans are national in scope and the other plans are local.

The payroll auditor who has to audit out-of-town employers will incur travel costs. These travel costs can be shared if the auditor can perform the same audit for unrelated plans, or if the auditor can schedule payroll audits for employers covered by other plans in the same geographic area.

Short-Term Report or No-Change Report

Some payroll audits result in no deficiencies or in very small deficiencies. In those instances it may be cost beneficial not to have the auditor produce a normal report with schedules attached (as described in Chapter 16). Instead, a single page report (for an example, see Exhibit F) may be sufficient for all parties.

Tips for Trustees

If your payroll auditor has to travel for payroll audits, make arrangements with other plans having employers in the same area to have the same auditor conduct both sets of audits at the same time. The resulting savings in travel costs can be dramatic.

Chapter 6

Finding and Retaining the Ideal Payroll Auditor

One reason plans give for not performing their own payroll audits internally is that finding and keeping payroll auditors is very difficult. What makes a person an excellent payroll auditor? What problems does the employer face in obtaining and retaining quality payroll auditors?

Qualities of the Payroll Auditor

Understands the Payroll Audit Process

The ideal payroll auditor understands the payroll audit process. The payroll audit is a compliance audit. The payroll auditor ensures that the employer is complying with the collective bargaining agreement (CBA) and is auditing the employer's payroll records searching for deficiencies. The payroll audit, by necessity, is much narrower in scope than a financial audit measuring the fairness of the financial statements. The efficient payroll auditor instinctively understands the difference in these two types of audit and will not spend needless time on audit procedures not relevant to the payroll audit process.

Quick

Auditors are trained to be methodical and thorough. They are taught to approach an audit by beginning at the first step and performing each and every audit step in the audit program, from beginning to end, in a logical and rational manner. An auditor trained in this manner may be a good auditor but may not be a good payroll auditor. The efficient payroll auditor attacks the audit from a "big picture" point of view. The efficient payroll auditor asks: "How can I get this job accomplished in the minimum amount of time while identifying the maximum deficiency, and if there is no deficiency, will I be smart enough to realize it quickly, finish up and get out?" The efficient payroll auditor doesn't waste anyone's time or money.

Enthusiastic

An excellent attribute for a payroll auditor is enthusiasm. Payroll audits can be tedious. Working conditions are not always ideal. The employer does not welcome the payroll auditor with open arms. The travel involved to and from the employer can be tiring. The auditor, who, in spite of all these problems, can remain cheerful and positive will do a better job and will last longer as a payroll auditor than one who is always unhappy about everything associated with the job.

Structured

The work performed by the payroll auditor at the employer's office may be done quickly. Then the auditor hurries to the next job and then the next and then rushes back to the office to write audit reports. Unless the auditor is a structured individual who keeps information filed in a logical and rational manner, the payroll audit will turn out to be a disaster. A good payroll auditor recognizes there will be times where the payroll audit will be put aside for a time period while other matters are attended to. The structured auditor knows where to go to restart the job efficiently and advance it toward completion.

Decisive

An efficient payroll auditor is a decision maker. Many decisions must be made in the payroll audit process. The efficient payroll auditor understands that making the right audit decisions without procrastination or indecisiveness leads to a quality payroll audit report.

TIPS FOR TRUSTEES

The payroll auditor in the field should always have someone to call during field work. One common question is whether the auditor should wrap up field work or return to the employer for a second day. Having someone with whom to discuss the situation normally results in the correct decision being made.

Doesn't Sweat the Small Stuff

The quality payroll auditor refuses to spend time on unimportant matters. A wise man once said, "Let little things be little things." An auditor can spend so much time on the unimportant issues that little time is devoted to those issues that are important to the payroll audit process.

Learner and Adaptor

Every good payroll auditor with whom the authors have ever been associated learns from his or her mistakes and adapts quickly to the situation. The auditor utilizes the lessons learned in these situations to decide how he or she will do things differently (i.e., hopefully in a more efficient manner) the next time he or she is faced with a similar situation.

A PAYROLL AUDITOR'S STORY

"One of my co-workers in payroll auditing had four or five payroll audits scheduled in a large midwestern state. He flew from point to point renting a new car in each location. He wasted a lot of time waiting for airplane flights, and it was very expensive. The audits would have been done more efficiently if he had flown to a central location and driven from audit to audit."

—*Larry Beebe*

Has Spreadsheet Skills

Before the advent of the personal computer, a great deal of time was spent in the payroll audit process copying information from one source to another. Not only did this take time, it often led to errors.

In the modern world of computer technology, payroll auditors should only have to write the information once and then use the power of the computer to transfer it any place needed. (Chapter 16 discusses how to use the computer efficiently in a payroll audit.) Computer technology only works if the person using the computer for the payroll audit makes maximum use of the available technology. The efficient payroll auditor is always looking for ways to use the computer to aid the overall audit effort.

The authors have listed those attributes believed to be essential for the efficient payroll auditor. Are there other attributes that might be helpful? Can a payroll auditor succeed without having all of these attributes? Can a payroll auditor who has most of these attributes still fail? The answer to each of these questions is *yes.* Working with payroll auditors, perhaps trustees will develop their own list of attributes. There is no magic formula for the perfect payroll auditor. The authors would be happy to hear from others who can improve on this list of attributes.

TIPS FOR TRUSTEES

When hiring a payroll auditor, look for a person with ambition, even if the ambition has nothing to do with payroll auditing. For example, a candidate for the position might say, "I want to own my own business someday." A person with this ambition is likely to be highly motivated and will be a self-starter. You might not keep this person as long as you keep other payroll auditors, but it is likely to be a positive experience for both parties as long as it lasts.

Employer Problems in Retaining the Payroll Auditor

The ideal payroll auditor has just been described. There are problems from the employers' prospective, however, in getting and keeping quality payroll auditors.

Pay Scale

Payroll auditors normally do not make a great deal of money. A payroll audit is a very labor-intensive process and cannot bear the cost of a high-priced auditor. Since the pay is not attractive to a skilled auditor, the person hired as a payroll auditor is not often an educated or trained accountant. Often the best payroll auditor is the inexperienced person who is unskilled, but is eager to learn and hopes to use the experience as a springboard to future success.

Travel

The payroll auditor won't spend a great amount of time in the office. The auditor normally will travel extensively, visiting employers in the area covered by the CBA. If the covered area is large enough, this may mean extensive out-of-town travel for the payroll auditor. If a person wants to work out of the office and/or out of town, this could make the payroll audit position more attractive than it would normally be if the pay were higher.

Tips for Trustees

Rotate the travel assignments so that every payroll auditor gets some of the good trips and some of the less desirable trips. A trip that most auditors might not like could be desirable for another auditor because that person has family in the area.

Confrontation Factor

The payroll auditor normally receives a cordial reception from the employer. The auditor must realize, however, that he or she is about as welcome as an IRS auditor. Since the payroll auditor looks for deficiencies, it makes him or her even less popular. The payroll auditor may often be confronted by an unhappy employer that cannot be placated. The payroll auditor cannot be confrontational in return. The payroll auditor must be friendly at all times even when informing the employer of the deficiencies found. Some auditors are not good payroll auditors because they can't be polite, but firm, with the employer.

Working Conditions

Ideally, the contributing employer being audited should provide reasonable workspace and working conditions to perform the audit. The payroll auditor quickly learns that ideal space and working conditions are far from reality. Often the payroll auditor is assigned the worst working space that an employer has. Every experienced payroll auditor can tell story after story about poor working conditions. There is little the auditor can do except grin and bear it. Unacceptable working conditions, however, should be challenged, and if they remain unchanged the auditor should be prepared to complain to the plan administrator or to the plan's legal counsel. A good payroll auditor gets the job done regardless of working conditions.

Poor working conditions are not the same as unsafe conditions. For the auditor's protection, the payroll audit supervisor and the auditor's office should know where the auditor is at all times. An auditor should report any unsafe working conditions immediately and should withdraw from the premises unless the conditions are promptly rectified. The audit may have to be rescheduled at a later date in the office of the employer's attorney or CPA.

In those rare instances where the auditor is threatened, intimidated or offered a bribe by the employer, the auditor should immediately withdraw and notify the supervisor or the plan attorney.

A Payroll Auditor's Story

"I once did a payroll audit in an eastern industrial city. I had been told that the employer had an explosive temper. This was clearly evident when within the first 20 minutes that I was there, he was verbally abusive to his employees. Within 30 minutes it was my turn. He challenged my right to copy information on unreported employees. I did not back down and terminated the audit when he would not cooperate any further. Within six months I was back, accompanied by a government attorney, and I found a very large deficiency."

—*Larry Beebe*

What Does the Future Hold for a Payroll Auditor?

Payroll audit positions can be dead-end jobs. Often the only chance of advancement is to progress to the payroll audit supervisor.

With all of these problems, how can the employer hope to retain and motivate payroll auditors? One way is to offer to pay the payroll auditor a bonus based on successful completion of a certain period on the job. Another "carrot or stick" is to promise the payroll auditor that upon satisfactory completion of a certain period of time as a payroll auditor, the person will be promoted to the regular audit staff (where that person works for a CPA firm) or to the regular internal audit staff (where that person works for the plan or a non-CPA firm employer). It is important for the payroll audit supervisor to have regular communication with the payroll audit staff regarding their future in the organization.

Chapter 7

Training the Payroll Auditor

Hiring the ideal payroll auditor solves one of the trustees' problems. Now the auditor must be trained before he or she can begin producing quality audit reports.

Understanding the Collective Bargaining Agreement (CBA)

The CBA serves as the contractual agreement between the plan and the contributing employers. The payroll auditor should thoroughly read the CBA to gain an understanding of:

- Employees covered by the CBA (and in some instances, descriptions of employees not covered)
- Wage rates and benefits to be paid in accordance with the CBA
- A determination of whether the benefit rates are for hours paid, hours worked or a percentage of gross wages
- Whether apprentices are covered and at what rate
- Whether payments are for all amounts paid, or whether there are exclusions such as a maximum of 40 hours paid per week, or whether vacation and holiday hours are to be included in calculating the amounts due.

Understanding the Jurisdiction

When all employees for a given employer work in the same location such as a factory building, a hotel or a bakery, the payroll auditor normally must determine only if the employee is covered by the CBA. Most covered employees in this instance, working in the same trade, are represented by the same local union. The employer pays the wage rates and fringe benefits for that local union.

There are circumstances, however, where the employer conducts business over a wide geographic area. For example, an employer, XYZ Company (XYZ), takes a job 200 miles away in another state. The job will cover 15 workers in the trade covered by the CBA. The employer takes five workers with him from his home Local Union A and employs ten other workers in the same trade from Local Union B at the jobsite.

The payroll auditor for the plans sponsored by Local Union A performs a payroll audit six months later. For that particular job, XYZ should have reported five of the workers to the plans sponsored by Local Union A, and the other ten employees to the plans sponsored by Local Union B. The plans in the two areas normally have a reciprocity agreement to cover this arrangement. The payroll auditor must understand when reciprocity agreements exist and should consider their provisions in performing the payroll audit.

There are times when all the individuals working for an employer are represented by the same union. There are other times when many different trades are working for the same employer. When the employer employs personnel working in many trades, a code is normally assigned to each employee by the employer that can be utilized by the payroll auditor to eliminate those employees not covered by the CBA. The auditor can also ask to see the remittance reports filed for other trades to eliminate those employees not covered by the CBA covering the plan he or she is auditing.

Difference Between a Financial Statement Audit and the Payroll Audit

The payroll audit is not a financial audit. It is a compliance audit. The payroll auditor wants to determine how well the employer is doing in complying with the reporting requirements as set forth by the CBA. Payroll auditors, who are experienced in financial statement auditing, often approach the payroll audit in the same manner as a financial statement audit. These auditors want to bring the proof mentality to payroll auditing. In a payroll audit, proving numbers such as gross payroll, is most often a waste of time. There are often faster and cheaper methods of ensuring compliance in a payroll audit.

Understanding the Objective

Just as auditors rely on sampling in a financial statement audit, a payroll auditor can rely on sampling in a payroll audit. A payroll auditor does not and should not audit every transaction to gain confidence that the employer is reporting in compliance with the CBA. If a payroll auditor conducts sufficient tests, those areas where errors are likely in a payroll audit should be revealed. If the auditor then spreads those tests over the time period to be tested and finds no errors, then further testing is not likely to find significant numbers of errors. An excellent payroll auditor develops a sixth sense of whether additional testing will uncover deficiencies. There is nothing wrong with relying on that experienced auditor's sixth sense.

A Payroll Auditor's Story

"I went to do a payroll audit where the contribution reports showed an average of 20 production-type employees being reported. When I arrived at the employer's location, the size of the plant was enormous. How could a plant this large only be reporting 20 employees? Immediately I began to look for unreported employees. The audit findings showed a deficiency of over $200,000."

—*Phil Vivirito*

The "Get In and Get Out" Mentality

The Peter Principle states that work expands to fill the time available for its completion. Nowhere is this truer than in a payroll audit. A payroll audit scheduled for a day of field work will almost always take one day to complete. The wise payroll audit supervisor recognizes this and attempts to adopt a "get in and get out" philosophy as an approach to efficient payroll auditing. The payroll audit supervisor should attempt to schedule two or more smaller employers on the same day to promote efficiency. Payroll auditors should be encouraged to work quickly and use the hours available at the end of the day to write their reports. Other timesaving techniques are discussed in Chapter 9.

Understanding the Relationship of Audit Cost to Findings

The goal of any payroll audit program should be to make money for the plan. A truly successful payroll audit program collects more in delinquencies and deficiencies than the cost of the payroll audit program. This may not be possible in a situation where there has been an aggressive payroll audit program for many years. Someone should be charged with the responsibility of annually measuring the monetary results of the payroll audit program. If revenue derived from the program is increasing compared to costs on a year-to-year basis, then more payroll audits should be scheduled. If the revenue is decreasing as a percentage of costs from year to year, then fewer payroll audits should be scheduled.

Chapter 8

Roles of the Parties Involved

The key parties in a payroll audit are payroll auditors themselves, the trustees of the plan and the external certified public accountants (CPAs) who audit the financial statements of the plan. Each of these parties has an essential role in the payroll audit process.

Role of the External Auditor

The financial statements of an employee benefit plan are the responsibility of the plan's management. The board of trustees of the plan is the plan's management. The external CPAs are hired by the board of trustees to audit the financial statements on an annual basis. All employee benefit plans with more than 100 participants are required to have this annual audit.

Statements on Auditing Standards, published by the American Institute of Certified Public Accountants (AICPA), say that there are certain assertions or representations by management "that are embodied in financial statement components." The standards then list the assertions, one of which is completeness. In other words, management is representing to the auditor that the financial statements contain everything that they should contain.

As part of determining that the financial statements are complete, the external auditor must be satisfied that the plan has received all of the income it should have received. Since the major portion of an employee benefit plan's income is employer contributions, the CPA must be satisfied that all employer contributions have been identified, reported, recorded and disclosed.

The easiest way to verify that employer contributions are accurate would seem to be the act of confirming in writing with the employer all contributions paid in the year being audited. There are two major problems with utilizing confirmations of employer contributions. The first is that the employer is unlikely to verify the information in the form and then return it. The second problem is that, even if the employer returns the confirmation, it only confirms what the employer has actually paid. The confirmation makes no representations about amounts that should have been paid, but were not. The confirmation may be a useful audit tool, but more needs to be done to verify the completeness of employer contributions.

In order to ensure that all employers are paying all amounts due under the collective bargaining agreement (CBA), the CPA would have to test the internal controls of each and every contributing employer to ensure that systems were in place to remit all amounts due under the terms of the CBA.

No multiemployer plan in existence could afford to direct its external auditor to test the controls of all contributing employers.

In lieu of testing controls, the external auditor should ensure that the plan is utilizing an adequate payroll audit program to periodically test the employer's compliance with the CBA. The external auditor must be satisfied that whoever is performing the payroll audits on the books and records of the contributing employers is performing the job in such a manner that the completeness objective has been achieved and an unqualified opinion can be given on the plan's financial statements.

The plan's external auditor may not be the plan's payroll auditor. In those circumstances, the external auditor should thoroughly review and document the payroll audit process. As part of this review process, the external auditor should select a representative sample of the payroll audits performed and review the thoroughness of the payroll audit process to ensure that sufficient, appropriate information has been obtained concerning the completeness of employer contributions.

Role of the Payroll Auditor

The payroll auditor has the central role in the payroll audit process. In fulfilling their roles in the process, the external auditor and the trustees depend on the adequacy and thoroughness of the work performed by the payroll auditor. The payroll auditor must properly complete the audit program (Chapter 5), which may be unique to the industry serviced by the plan, and should also accomplish the following tasks on each of the payroll audits performed:

1. **Ensure that the employer is asked for all needed records in advance.** Normally the plan writes a letter to the employer (see example in Appendix C) stating that he or she has been selected for a payroll audit. The letter should inform the employer exactly what records must be available on the date of the audit. Upon arrival, the auditor should ensure that all needed records are available.
2. **Understand how the employer's payroll system operates.** The auditor should, upon arrival at the employer, gain a quick understanding of how the payroll system operates. This is often accomplished by questioning the employer's accounting personnel and by testing one or more regularly reported employees. It is also important that the auditor understand how the payroll system records overtime and how that overtime is reflected on the remittance report.
3. **Identify covered and noncovered employees.** Often the employer codes employees by type. The auditor, with the aid of the employer's representative, should gain an understanding of which codes represent reportable employees.

A Payroll Auditor's Story

"As soon as I arrive at an employer, I ask to see all of the records that were requested in the letter sent by the plan. If any of the records have not been produced, I make a list of the missing items and give it to the employer with an explanation that if any of the records are not produced during my visit, I will have to inform the plan's attorney. It is amazing how fast the missing records appear."

—Tom Seay

Tips for Payroll Auditors

Asking the employer for remittance report files for other union plans is often a good way to eliminate nonreportable employees, unless there is some dispute as to whether the plan being audited has responsibility for those employees.

4. **Look for deficiencies.** The primary responsibility of a payroll auditor is to ensure that the employer is reporting properly to the plan. The easiest way for the auditor to fulfill this responsibility is to look for deficiencies. If no deficiencies are found, the auditor has gained assurance that the employer is reporting properly. If deficiencies are found in the audit testing, the sampling performed can be expanded to determine the extent of the deficiencies for that employer.
5. **Document the thought process.** In Chapter 5 the authors urged the use of a flexible audit program by the payroll auditor. In order for a flexible audit approach to work, the auditor must explain why certain steps in the audit program have been performed, and why other steps have been omitted. The auditor does this by documenting his or her thought process during the course of the performance of the payroll audit. If the thought process of the auditor is properly documented at the time the audit is performed, it is difficult for anyone to challenge the auditor as to the thoroughness of the job performed.
6. **Know when to leave and know when to come back.** The payroll auditor must learn to know how to use time efficiently. An essential decision, which must be made in most audits, is whether to complete all of the field work on the first day, or to come back to the employer for a second day. Unless deficiencies are being found, the auditor should not normally come back for a second day. This is explored more fully in Chapter 9, which discusses saving audit and travel time.
7. **Communicate with the employer.** Most plans require the auditor to discuss the results of the payroll audit with the employer or his or her representative in an exit interview. The exit interview allows the employer an opportunity to present additional evidence as to why certain amounts should not be shown as deficiencies or errors. When the employer receives the written payroll audit report it will not be a surprise.
8. **Prepare the report in a timely manner.** Performing the field work can be the easy part of the payroll audit.

Tips for Trustees

The payroll auditor should attempt to hold the exit interview with a person at the employer who has the authority to make a decision to either accept or reject the auditor findings. Many times the employer wants a person with little or no authority to communicate with the auditor. This may be sufficient for providing information during the audit, but the exit interview should be held with a person at the highest level of responsibility possible.

Finding the time to write the report on a timely basis once the field work is completed is often difficult. The key to timely report preparation is scheduling the field work. Timely report delivery satisfies everyone concerned with the audit.

Role of the Trustees

The trustees have the ultimate responsibility for conducting a well-run payroll audit program. The specific steps that the trustees generally have in the collection process, and specifically in the payroll audit program, include:

1. **Collect all contributions due to the plan.** One of the responsibilities of a plan's trustees is to collect all employer contributions due to the plan. The trustees can ensure that they fulfill this responsibility by conducting an efficient and effective payroll audit program. The payroll auditor often decides which specific steps to perform in an audit, and often has a role in selecting which specific employers are to be audited in a given payroll audit cycle. The trustees, however, are ultimately responsible for the entire payroll audit program as one of the essential steps in the collection of employer contributions.
2. **Allow no loans or extensions of credit.** ERISA, in Section 406(c)(1)(b), states that a plan cannot lend money or extend credit between itself and a party in interest. A contributing employer is a party in interest, and a failure to collect employer contributions can be construed as a loan or extension of credit. A failure of the trustees to collect all contributions due to the plan can also be construed to be a loan or extension of credit. A payroll audit program does not ensure that all employer contributions are collected, but such a program, effectively and efficiently operated, demonstrates that the trustees are not knowingly granting loans or extensions of credit to employers.
3. **Satisfy the rule of prudence.** Ultimately the trustees of a plan are judged as to whether they are acting with prudence. Are the trustees acting in the same or similar manner as other trustees would in attempting to collect all monies due to the plan for employer contributions? Without having payroll audits performed, it is extremely difficult for the trustees to determine whether employer contributions are made to the plan. Prudent trustees have a payroll audit program.
4. **Allow no employer a competitive advantage.** Payroll auditors find that employer trustees are just as aggressive as union trustees in insisting that payroll audits be performed. Why? No employer wants to be placed at a competitive disadvantage. If an employer doesn't pay the required fringe benefits, that employer has an economic advantage compared to employers that pay for all of their required contributions to employee benefit plans. To ensure compliance with the provisions of the CBA, employer trustees often insist their own companies be audited as part of the payroll audit program.
5. **Have an appeal process for collection of employer contributions.** If an employer is late with a contribution, that employer should have the right to appeal any penalties imposed.

Tips for Trustees

Normally an employer should not have the right to appeal interest imposed on late employer contributions. The plan was entitled to receive employer contributions on a timely basis, and interest is to reimburse the plan for investment earnings not received because of the failure to receive timely employer contributions.

When payroll audits are performed, the payroll auditor may be uncertain as to whether hours (and or wages) for certain employees are subject to the CBA. When in doubt, after trying to verify with the employees in question which employees are subject to the CBA, the auditor includes the hours (or wages) for these employees as deficiencies in the payroll audit report. The trustees, as part of the appeals process, can offer the employer the right to offer additional, final evidence as to why these employees should not be reported.

The trustees often delegate their authority to collect employer contributions and perform payroll audits to the administrator of the plan. The trustees should receive regular reports from the payroll auditors, the administrator and legal counsel in charge of collections as to the status of the payroll audit program. Ultimately, the responsibility for the payroll audit rests with the trustees. The trustees have to decide if all those responsible for the collection of employer contributions and payroll audits are doing their jobs.

Chapter 9

Saving Audit and Travel Time

Some employee benefit plans have all of their contributing employers located in a small geographic area where little or no travel time is required for the payroll auditor. Other employee benefit plans have their contributing employers spread out in wide geographical areas (perhaps even the entire country), and the payroll auditor must make a conscientious effort to avoid wasting travel time in performing the audit.

Not all timesaving techniques in a payroll audit deal with travel time. Time saving can also be a result of proper scheduling techniques, efficient audit techniques, using the computer effectively and effective report writing. Chapters 13 and 14 are devoted to using the computer and writing the report. This entire book is an attempt to promote efficient audit techniques in a payroll audit. This chapter discusses saving time in scheduling and performing the audit, and in travel time during the course of the audit. In Appendix G there are 20 tips for out-of-town payroll audits.

Chapter 4 discussed the necessary steps in scheduling the audit. Once the audit is scheduled, there are certain steps the payroll auditor can perform that can save time before the audit field work starts.

1. Letter of introduction. The auditor should have a letter of introduction from the plan administrator confirming the auditor's identity. This letter will often cite the authority under the agreement and declaration of trust to perform the audit. Presenting this letter to the employer as soon as the payroll auditor enters the employer's premises can save time. For a sample letter, see Appendix C.
2. Locate the employer the night before the audit starts. If the auditor has to travel out of town to the audit, he or she will often arrive in the area the night before the audit begins. Traveling to and locating the employer the night before the audit starts may save precious audit time the next day. The auditor can also call the employer the day before the audit to ensure the directions he or she has are accurate—even if the auditor has a global positioning system (GPS), which should pinpoint the location exactly. Calling to learn the nuances of locating the employer has its advantages.
3. Make sure that the employer has produced all of the records asked for as soon as the auditor arrives. If this is done early in the process, the employer has time to produce the "missing item(s)" before the auditor leaves.
4. Have copies (on the payroll auditor's computer) of the remittance reports

A Payroll Auditor's Story

"I flew into a southern U.S. city on a Sunday afternoon. A freak snowstorm hit the area and I finally arrived at my hotel. When I arrived at the employer's premises the next morning, they had no power and had no prospect of getting it back that day. I called several of the employers that I had scheduled for later in the week and finally found one that had managed to get to work. He was the only person who had gotten to the office and he let me come and do the audit. I managed to reschedule all of my audits and finished on schedule."

—Larry Beebe

filed by the employer for the period covered by the payroll audit. This can save time if the employer disputes the plan's record of any remittance reports and/or payments sent.

5. Schedule two audits in one day, if possible. Normally, if an employer has 40 or fewer employees and the audit period covers no more than three years, the audit can be completed in a half-day or less. If the payroll auditor is traveling out of town, two small audits should be scheduled for one day. One audit can be done in the morning and the second can be done in the afternoon. When scheduling the second audit of the day, the auditor should tell the employer that there may be a chance that the audit will have to be rescheduled if the first audit takes too much time. For each audit scheduled later in the week, the employer should be told that the payroll audit might have to be rescheduled. Performing the field work on two or more employers in one day can be a tremendous time saver for the payroll auditor.

Performing the Detailed Audit Work

The payroll auditor should not approach the payroll audit in the same manner in which a financial statement auditor approaches an audit. The goal of a financial statement audit is to ensure that the financial statements are presented fairly. The financial statement auditor has to prove many different amounts and accounts in making that judgment.

The financial statement auditor will normally bring this "proof mentality" to the payroll audit process. The goal of the payroll auditor is not to "prove" the employer's payroll. The goal of the payroll auditor is to ensure the contributing employer's compliance with the collective bargaining agreement (CBA) and to search for deficiencies.

The auditor can save time in performing the payroll audit by doing the following:

1. **Look for deficiencies.** Once the payroll auditor understands how the system works by checking hours reported for several employees, most of the audit testing should be directed

Tips for Payroll Auditors

Ask if the person preparing the remittance reports has a system to ensure that all hours that should be reported, are reported. Finding that such a system exists and determining that it works properly could save a great deal of time in the audit of a large employer.

toward identifying audit deficiencies. The auditor should test those areas where deficiencies are likely (see Chapter 10) and expand testing when deficiencies are found. Once most or all of the deficiencies have been found, the auditor should end the field work portion of the audit.

2. **Question the employer's representative.** Spending time with the employer's representative in determining how the payroll system operates and how the remittance reports are prepared can save the auditor time.
3. **Assess the surroundings.** An experienced auditor can often sense, after a short period of time, whether deficiencies are likely to be found at an employer. This assessment can be based on the business atmosphere at the employer, the helpfulness of the employer's staff and a determination of whether the employer is cooperating in the audit. As the work progresses, the original assessment of the surroundings may not prove to be valid but most often it does.
4. **Scan the cash disbursements journal.** The employer knows that the payroll auditor will review the payroll records and is likely to find any deficiencies or shortages in those records. Therefore, some employers are likely to disguise payments for labor in a different category in the general ledger. The most likely charge for these hours is the category of subcontract labor. Other employers will try to totally disguise the payments by charging these payments to materials or other unrelated general ledger categories such as travel and entertainment.
5. **Check tips from covered employees, other employers and union officials.** Tips from interested parties often lead to the identification of large payroll audit deficiencies. Once the payroll auditor knows what should have been reported, it is easy to determine the deficiencies involved.
6. **Call the fund attorney or fund administrator from the field to ask for advice.** Employers often ask questions the payroll auditor is not qualified to answer, or the payroll auditor needs the expertise of others in doing the job. The payroll auditor should not be reluctant to pick up the phone and ask for help.
7. **Timecards.** In certain industries, employees are required to keep timecards. How can the payroll auditor be sure that the employer is reporting correctly unless the timecards are audited? Most often auditing timecards is a waste of audit time. If an employee is not being paid for the correct number of hours, that employee is likely to complain. Unless someone alleges that there is a problem with the timecards, they should most likely receive only minimal scrutiny. In many instances, they can be ignored.

Tips for Payroll Auditors

Ask to see invoices supporting subcontract payments and other charges that come to the payroll auditor's attention. If the payroll auditor becomes convinced that any of these payments are actually payments for hours subject to the CBA, then these amounts can be converted to hours by dividing the gross amount paid by the most common wage rate in the CBA.

A Payroll Auditor's Story

"We received a tip from a disgruntled employee. He said that the employer was disguising payments to him for covered employment by writing checks to the liquor store the employee owned. I found numerous payments to the liquor store coded in the cash disbursements journal as 'travel and entertainment.' When these payments were converted to hours paid, a substantial underpayment deficiency was assessed and collected."

—Tom Seay

8. **Scan rather than test in detail.** The experienced payroll auditor knows how to scan the employer's payroll and accounting records searching for deficiencies. Scanning the records is often a better technique than detailed testing, because the payroll auditor spends less time on routine transactions that are likely not to have errors.
9. **Unreported fractional hours.** The auditor may find minor deficiencies, such as unreported fractional hours, that have a minimal financial impact on the employer's reporting. The plan is best served having these minimal deficiencies brought to the attention of the employer with the insistence that they be correctly reported in the future. The payroll auditor can spend many hours on this type of minor deficiency, which results in a waste of the plan's resources.

Finishing the Field Work

Determining when to finish the field work is often difficult for the payroll auditor. How does the payroll auditor know that he or she has found all of the deficiencies that he or she should find? The simple answer is the payroll auditor never knows the answer to that question. The experienced payroll auditor knows that deciding when to end field work often saves considerable time in the audit.

If the payroll auditor is out of town and decides to end the field work, it doesn't necessarily mean that the day is ended. The payroll auditor should take a ride to the site of the next employer to make sure it can be found. The payroll auditor should go back to the hotel and start writing the audit report. Or he or she can make phone calls to the payroll audit supervisor or to the plan. There is always something productive to do in the world of payroll auditing.

Tips for Trustees

In some building trade industries, the trustees ask the payroll auditor to compare total amounts paid by the employer for materials and for wages. If materials are too high in relation to wages, the assumption is made that the employer has disguised wages as materials.

Chapter 10

Deficiencies

The primary role of the payroll auditor is to verify that the employer being audited is complying with the terms of the collective bargaining agreement (CBA). The payroll auditor must also perform the audit in such a manner that if delinquencies and deficiencies exist they will be identified and collected.

Deficiencies and Delinquencies

What is the difference between a delinquency and a deficiency in a payroll audit? A *delinquency* exists when the employer acknowledges liability for the amounts owed for prior periods but has not yet remitted the funds to the plan. How does the payroll auditor find out about delinquencies? First, the payroll auditor asks the plan to furnish information for any periods for which the employer has not remitted contributions. Upon arrival at the employer, the auditor should ask if any unpaid amounts for prior periods are due to the plan.

Deficiencies are typically revealed as a result of the payroll audit. The payroll auditor discovers that the employer has not paid for all amounts that should have been paid had the CBA been strictly adhered to. Some deficiencies are routine in nature and are easily identified, while other deficiencies are more difficult to identify.

Normal Deficiencies

Routine deficiencies that should be easily identified by the payroll auditor include:

1. **Clerical errors.** The employer fails to report the correct number of hours for a covered employee. For example, an employee works 40 hours in a given week and the employer only remits for and pays for 35 hours.
2. **New employees.** The employer fails to report new employees as soon as is required by the CBA.
3. **Terminating employees.** The employer fails to report employees in their last days of employment.
4. **Overtime.** The employer fails to report overtime hours paid to employees. Some CBAs only require reporting 40 hours per week, while other CBAs require reporting all hours paid.
5. **Paid vacations and holidays.** Some CBAs only require the reporting of hours worked. In those situations, vacation and holiday hours paid would not be reported because they are not hours worked. However, in those situations where the CBA

requires reporting all hours paid, then vacation and holiday hours should be reported.

6. **Sick pay and bonuses.** Some CBAs do not require the reporting of sick pay and bonuses. Other CBAs state that hours for sick pay and bonuses must be reported. A payroll auditor might be confronted with bonuses paid where the employer will not convert the bonus to hours paid. Normally the auditor would convert the bonus to hours paid by dividing the gross bonus by the prevailing wage rate in the CBA.
7. **Apprentices.** Some CBAs do not require reporting of hours worked by apprentices, while other CBAs do require the reporting of these hours. Some CBAs require making contributions at the same hourly rates for both journeymen and apprentices, while other CBAs discount the hourly rate paid for apprentices. Often the proper handling of apprentices is confusing and this often leads to deficiencies.
8. **Covered nonunion employees.** An employer may operate under the mistaken impression that remittances to the plan do not have to be made for nonunion employees. Whether the employee is or is not a union member is not relevant for reporting purposes. The general rule is that all hours paid (or worked) must be reported for all employees working in a job covered by the CBA.
9. **Subcontracted or leased employees.** An employer normally cannot escape its obligation under the CBA by hiring a subcontractor or leased employee. Employers often operate under the mistaken assumption that they do not have to report such individuals.
10. **Fifth week of a month.** An employer may carefully record all four weeks worked by its employees on the monthly remittance report. That same employer may forget that every third month has five weeks since there are 13 weeks in a calendar quarter.
11. **Employee status.** Some CBAs have different requirements based on whether an employee is full time or part time. There may be different waiting periods to begin contributions or a different contribution rate.
12. **Capping.** There may be a cap or limit on how many hours upon which an employer must contribute. The cap may be weekly or daily. Some employers may erroneously prorate units or fail to contribute on certain pay types such as overtime and vacation.

A Payroll Auditor's Story

"I was performing an audit on the records of a company that was ceasing operations. The employer stated that current year payroll records were unavailable and that all covered employees had been terminated in the previous year. On the way to the restroom I noticed a time clock. I grabbed a pad and wrote down the names on the timecards. I informed the employer that I knew that covered employees were still working. The payroll records for the current year suddenly appeared and I was able to calculate the deficiency owed."

—*Phil Vivirito*

Unusual Deficiencies

Most of the deficiencies noted above are routine in nature and can be the result of an honest mistake or misinterpretation of the CBA. Unfortunately, there are some employers that deliberately attempt to avoid their legitimate obligations under the CBA by disguising their payments to covered employees. Some of the methods used by these employers include:

1. **Disguising hours paid as expenses.** An expense that is listed as supplies, entertainment, and truck or equipment rental or in any other expense category can actually be a payment for wages that are subject to reporting under the CBA. Unfortunately, such deliberate misclassification of expense is almost impossible for the auditor to prove. A complaint from a disgruntled employee may be the only way to find this type of deficiency.
2. **Disguising hours paid as materials.** Materials can be the largest expense paid by an employer. Therefore, the unscrupulous employer may believe that wage payments can be buried in this expense category. In some building trades, payroll auditors are instructed to calculate a ratio between wages and materials. If the calculated ratio exceeds a certain predetermined maximum, the excess amount paid by materials is considered to be wages paid and the employer is billed for this deficiency when the payroll audit is performed.
3. **Disguising payments to subcontractors.** An employer may, subject to the terms of the CBA, legitimately utilize subcontractors to perform certain work. These subcontractors then have their own reporting requirements under the CBA. However, some payments to subcontractors may actually be payments made to employees to avoid payment of employer contributions. The payroll auditor should always scan payments shown under subcontracting expense in the employer's general ledger to determine if payments recorded there were handled correctly. If in doubt, the payroll auditor should ask to see the invoices submitted by the subcontractors.
4. **Alter ego.** The employer can attempt to avoid reporting under the CBA by starting another company. The alter ego company will be discussed in Chapter 14.
5. **Failure to report a covered group.** An employer may fail to report all groups of employees covered by the CBA. The payroll auditor should carefully review whom the employer is reporting and not reporting to determine if a covered class of employees is not being reported.
6. **Double set of books.** In very rare circumstances, the employer may have one legitimate set of books and another phony set of books to be shown to payroll auditors and the IRS. There is almost no way that an auditor could determine such a subterfuge.
7. **Payments off the books.** If the employer pays the employees in cash or in any other manner in which the payment is not shown on the company books, the chance that the payroll auditor will find this deficiency is almost nonexistent. The auditor can't find something that is not there.
8. **Retired employee returning to work.** Depending on the plan, retirees returning to a covered position may have to be contributed for, depending on how many hours they work.
9. **Owners.** A company's owner may or may not be required to be contributed

A Payroll Auditor's Story

"I once performed a payroll audit in a large southern city. The books were perfect, too perfect. When I questioned the bookkeeper, I found she knew almost nothing about the books that she was supposedly keeping. I found no deficiencies and was convinced that I was looking at a double set of books. When I later found that the employer was rumored to have ties to organized crime, I became convinced that I was indeed looking at a double set of books."

—*Tom Seay*

for, depending on the plan. Some building trades allow an owner working with tools to be contributed for, while other plans will not allow contributions for an owner.

10. **Nonbargaining employees and alumni.** There are plans that have participation agreements for a group of nonbargaining unit employees. Some plans have agreements that cover alumni, who are employees that were in the plan but are no longer working with tools of the trade. Deficiencies occur when an employer signs one of these agreements but doesn't follow it explicitly. An employer may pick and choose who gets reported as opposed to reporting everyone in these categories.
11. **Refunds.** The employer may state that it has overpaid and request a refund of amounts paid. (Once, the authors were assigned to check the validity of a $56,000 refund requested by an employer. The claim was valid, but enough deficiencies were found to reduce the refund paid to $8,000.)
12. **Bonuses.** Some payments to covered employees are categorized as bonuses for completion of work. In some instances, the bonuses are legitimate and do not represent hours paid. In other instances, however, the employer is really paying for hours worked and is attempting to avoid payment to the employee benefit plan.

Conclusion

Most of the deficiencies found by payroll auditors are in the categories noted above. Intelligent payroll auditors recognize, however, that if they do enough payroll audits they will eventually find something new or unusual.

Chapter 11

Contents of the Audit File

How does the payroll auditor set up a payroll audit file? What information should be included and where does it go? No matter how the file is set up, whether it is paper or electronic, there are certain items that must be included.

Following are the items that should be part of the payroll audit file:

Audit notification letter. This is the initial contact to an employer notifying it of the payroll audit. It usually comes from the plan. It states that the employer has been selected for an audit and it may cite the trust agreement and the plan's audit policy. It should state the auditor's name and that he or she will be contacting the employer to schedule the audit. Ideally it should list the records required for the audit. See Appendix C for a sample.

Letter of audit confirmation. Once the auditor has scheduled the audit, a letter confirming the appointment should be sent to the employer. It should confirm the date and time, as well as the records required to complete the audit. It will give the employer the auditor's contact information as well. This letter should be sent by registered mail, fax or e-mail. The idea is for the auditor to have proof that contact was made, an audit appointment set up and confirmation of such sent to the employer. A sample can be found in Appendix H.

Collective bargaining agreement (CBA). The audit file should have a copy of the CBA and any other similar documents such as participation agreements. The CBA should encompass the audit period, so at times there may be more than one CBA required for the audit. It is preferable to have the entire CBA, not just the pages dealing with the funds being audited. Sometimes the language dealing with the employer being audited may not be adequate without referencing another section of the CBA. For example, contributions may be required for all regular employees, but the definition of a *regular employee* may be in another portion of the CBA.

Agreement and declaration of trust. This is usually a large document and, unlike the CBA, the whole document need not be part of the audit file. The section of the agreement that allows for a payroll audit program of participating employers is sufficient. The entire agreement, however, should be readily available for the payroll auditor if and when the need arises.

History of contributions to the plan. For the audit period, this could be a recap by month showing total units and total dollars received by the plan from the employer being audited. This will show any delinquencies during the audit period, as well as variations in the size of the employer during the audit period.

Questionnaire regarding payroll system. This questionnaire was discussed in Chapter 4 and lists the questions that should be asked about an employer's payroll. Ideally, it should be completed prior to the start of field work. The auditor can send it via e-mail or with the audit confirmation letter and request it be faxed or e-mailed back. Having this filled out prior to the audit will help in planning the audit. The questionnaire identifies employer size, the type of payroll and the information contained within the payroll. The questionnaire will also tell how the employer is handling reporting different pay types such as vacations, overtime and holidays, as well as how new hires are handled. If the employer's answers are contrary to what is required by the CBA, the auditor can plan accordingly. Knowing this before entering the employer's office will greatly enhance the auditor's efficiency.

Audit program. The audit program acts as a guide and checklist for the auditor. It should take the auditor through all the necessary steps, from scheduling the audit right through submitting it for technical review.

The program should note when the notification and audit confirmation letters were sent, as well as if all requested records were made available to the auditor. If the records were not made available, the program should indicate why some may be missing. The audit program should then take the auditor through the audit testing. Each required test should be listed along with space for the auditor's notation on sample size. There should also be a listing of the results of each test. The program should ensure that the auditor checks for all possibilities of unreported employees and units. The program should also address any special requests made by the plan. Finally, it should ensure that the auditor conducts the appropriate exit interviews and submits the audit report correctly.

One other important piece of the program is the auditor's comments on the employer's reporting process and system. The auditor should detail this information and include references to working papers located elsewhere in the audit file. See Appendix J.

Key information regarding the employer. Anything that may affect the audit or how the auditor approaches the audit should be included; for example, correspondence between the plan and the employer as it relates to the contributions being made by the employer. Also, any correspondence between the local union and the employer that may clarify certain sections of the CBA should be included. Information should also be included if there has been a major expansion or reduction of the employer's business, or a change in ownership. If the employer was previously audited, those audit results should be included. Finally, information from the employer's Web site may be useful.

Directions to employer's location. This is an obvious piece of information that can save the auditor valuable time. Obtaining directions from the Internet will lay out the route and estimate travel time, but the auditor should also call the employer and verify the directions. There may be road construction or road closures that will affect travel. Also, the employer is the one who can tell the auditor where to park or how to access the building.

Pro forma audit report. This should be set up specifically for each plan that the auditor serves. In an Excel version, there should be a control sheet where the auditor can enter data about the employer, the plan and the CBA. Linked to the other pages, this will begin preparation of the audit report. The pro forma report should also contain the spreadsheets for any audit findings. This will allow the auditor to enter data and prepare the audit report while still in the field.

Remittance reports. Remittance reports or contribution reports for the audit period should list employees reported by the employer, with Social Security numbers, units reported and dollar amount. Usually there is one report per month. Depending on the capabilities of the plan, the auditor may obtain these reports either in paper format or electronic format. The most efficient way would be the electronic format. Remittance reports in electronic format can be manipulated by the auditor to fit the needs of the audit. Hard copies of remittance reports tend to slow the auditor down. For example, if the remittance reports are in alphabetical order and the payroll is in Social Security number order, the auditor will have to search for the individual in each remittance report. With an electronic file, a data sort will solve this problem.

Working papers. The working papers are the auditor's documentation of what tests were performed and the results of those tests. They also contain the auditor's conclusions on the employer's compliance with the CBA and the identification of any deficiencies discovered. The audit program, as mentioned earlier, lists the tests and audit steps and is where the documentation of the tests should be. The working papers may be created entirely by the auditor, or the remittance reports may become working papers. Often an audit file contains many types of working papers.

When using the remittance reports, whether paper or electronic, the auditor should use a series of audit tick marks to identify correctness of the report or errors discovered. Comments can also be added. The file of working papers should be well organized so the auditor can easily identify any deficiencies discovered. The working papers should also support the auditor's conclusion of why there are deficiencies, or why there are no deficiencies.

Any forms used for tests should have the goal of supporting the auditor's conclusions. A form for testing new hires and terminating employees can be found in Appendix K.

There are also instances where working papers will exist separate from the remittance reports and will have to be listed on separate forms. An example is a listing of individuals receiving Form 1099s from the employer. Another is a list of employees on payroll but not on the remittance reports. Once these lists are created, the auditor must determine if any individuals are performing covered work. Documentation of the findings must be included on these lists and then a conclusion as to whether there are deficiencies.

Items provided by the employer should also become part of the working papers. These could include a department code list, a hire/termination list, a listing of pay codes, a job classification list or a sample page from payroll.

Audit report. Finally, the audit file should contain the audit report. The report should be in a format agreed to by the plan. It should list any discrepancies discovered or state that none were discovered. Comments regarding the discrepancies can be useful to both the plan and the employer that was audited. Any findings on the audit report should be the ones the auditor identified in the working papers. The audit report is discussed further in Chapter 13.

Chapter 12

Using the Computer Efficiently

Templates

Payroll audit reports and working papers should be standardized. This helps both the auditor and the plan by having a pro forma template (e.g., in Excel) for all audits so that the plan auditor does not have to recreate spreadsheets and forms for each audit. The pro forma template should include at a minimum the basics for the audit, such as the yearly exception schedules, summary page and comment page. All of these should be formatted with formulas and style (e.g., width, font size, etc.) so the auditor only needs to enter data.

After a few audits, the use of the template will become second nature and allow the auditor to concentrate on the audit itself. The plan also benefits because it knows what type of report to expect from its auditors. When the auditor sends an electronic copy of the audit report to the plan, processing the reports will be much easier since the plan personnel are familiar with the report format. More importantly, there will be a cost savings as many steps become automated.

Ideally, the pro forma template for the audit report should contain features that will help the auditor be more efficient.

A control sheet should be created where basic information such as employer name, plan name, audit period, contribution rates and basis are entered. This information can be linked to the appropriate pages in the report. Questions in the audit program should have drop down boxes that will allow the auditor to click the appropriate answer. Comments and warnings can then pop up, depending on the answer chosen by the auditor, that help lead to the next step.

All spreadsheets should be formatted and formulas already put in place. If a particular plan requires findings grouped or totaled in a certain way, that audit template should be set up with the appropriate tools such as subtotals or pivot tables. If the report requires certain standard language or comments for audit findings, they should be placed into a menulike format so the auditor can pick the correct one and drop it into the audit report. This helps to maintain audit efficiency as well as make the audit reviewer's job easier.

Working papers should also be standardized. A defined set of tick marks should be used. In an electronic format, tick marks must be interactive. In a paper audit, a tick mark usually is a symbol that indicates a certain finding or correctness of an employer's contribution. A tick mark in an electronic form will do the same and more. It can, for example, be a letter in a separate column in the Excel spreadsheet. This is how the auditor will be able to sort or filter and isolate findings. If, for example, the letter "H" is used and defined as omitted holiday time, the auditor can use a filter to group all of the omitted holiday exceptions.

Comments may be inserted into cells, which can explain how findings were discovered or why certain hours are correct. By using color shading and highlighting certain information, the audit reviewer can be directed through the working papers. Finally, by hyperlinking the auditor findings to the working paper that documents the findings, the reviewer will have a clear trail.

File Formats

If the plan is able to provide electronic data for an audit, knowing what to request is extremely important. If the auditor is working in Excel and the plan can provide information in Excel, that's great. But if not, then what? The best thing is to request the data in a text file; then it can be delineated. However, the auditor must specify the data required for the audit. At the very least, the participant name, Social Security number, month, year and number of units reported are needed. The auditor should request that CBAs and other documents be sent electronically in pdf format. A meeting with a plan's information technology department before beginning an audit program will determine the extent of electronic data available.

The electronic file should be set up just as one would set up a paper file before going out into the field. Whatever can be put into the file, such as the information on the control sheet, should be done when scheduling the audit. Then the audit template is saved in the audit file.

A network file folder should be set up for each audit. In this file folder the auditor can save the audit template as the audit report. This file folder should also contain the CBA, electronic contribution data, audit notification letter, audit confirmation letter and other documents received from the plan. Audit working papers are also saved in this file folder. Any documents received from the employer should be scanned and saved here, as well as all e-mail correspondence with the employer. Naming all of the above should be standard procedure for every audit. This will avoid having to open several items to determine their content.

> **TIPS FOR PAYROLL AUDITORS**
>
> When referring to a document or another file, the item being referred to can be hyperlinked to a key word or phrase.

E-Mail

Corresponding via e-mail with the employer can help increase the auditor's efficiency. When scheduling the audit, ask for the contact person's e-mail address and e-mail them a copy of the audit confirmation letter and pre-audit questionnaire. By doing this, the auditor will have already streamlined the audit process. The auditor may even have questions regarding something on the contribution reports before going out to the field. An e-mail with the item in question attached may give the auditor vital information before beginning the audit. Also, if during field work there are some documents that the auditor requested from the employer, have the employer e-mail them.

Using Data in the Field

For field work, the auditor should make a copy of the electronic file folder and save it to his or her hard drive for the audit. This ensures that any original data is not compromised. The ideal situation is for the auditor to use the electronic contribution reports as working papers, with the best-case scenario being that the data is in an Excel format. In this way the auditor can sort and filter the data to fit the needs of the audit.

For example, if the payroll is in Social Security number order, the contribution reports can be sorted by Social Security number. By using filters, the auditor can pick out certain employees, months or even see just one employee for an entire year.

Just as a paper file has documentation and tick marks, so should the electronic file. The auditor should be able to isolate findings and errors, as well as note what makes up the units on the contribution report. Highlighting cells and using different colors for text can be used to draw attention to something; however, it will not enable the auditor to manipulate the data. Adding an extra column to the spreadsheet and entering a number or letter as a tick mark will allow the auditor to sort and filter the data. Comments can also be inserted into individual cells to document what units the employer is reporting. The more that data can be manipulated, the more efficient the audit. Therefore, it is important that the auditor knows and understands how to do this.

The auditor should have more than just a basic knowledge of Excel. When the situation arises, an audit may need to apply advanced filters, use pivot tables and even logic formulas to arrange the data in the most efficient format.

Tips for Payroll Auditors

When delineating the data, place the month and year in separate fields. This will give more options when filtering data.

Audit Completion

Once the audit is completed, the file needs to be saved to a secure location such as the payroll auditor's network. Audit reports sent out should be scanned and saved into the electronic file folder. The Excel audit report and working papers should be saved as read-only documents to avoid accidentally changing them. Organize the electronic file just like a paper file. Have a folder for correspondence, one for reports and one for working papers. File-saving rules and names should be consistent. This will ensure that files can be easily and quickly accessed when needed.

The payroll audit department should keep a database of all its payroll audits. It should track audits from when the department received them, through the schedule date, review date and date delivered to the plan. When maintaining information such as number of employees, audit period and which of the auditors the audit has been assigned to, the database becomes a powerful tool. It will allow the payroll audit manager to provide status reports for each plan being audited and aid in maintaining the payroll audit cycles and turnaround time of the audits. The manager can keep a close eye on audits that are taking too long. A backlog report can be produced not only for a particular plan, but also for a specific auditor.

When the audit is complete and ready for technical review, the reviewer should open the electronic file and review it from there. Formulas on the report can be easily checked, just as spelling can. However, it is important that the reviewer checks the documentation and working papers. Did the auditor capture all of the deficiencies from the working papers to the audit report? Are there enough comments to document the employer's reporting procedures? These questions can only be answered by opening the electronic file to check formulas, links and how the auditor manipulated data.

Chapter 13

Preparing an Audit Report

For each payroll audit performed, the payroll auditor will issue an audit report. What should be the contents of the audit report? Who prepares the report and when should it be prepared? The answers to these questions are discussed in this chapter.

Preparing the Audit Report in the Field

While still in the field, the payroll auditor should start the audit report. The first test the auditor should perform is to ensure that all covered employees are being reported. Any employee not reported should be identified. If the employer has a payroll grouped by department, this can be an easy task because entire departments of employees not covered by the CBA can be ruled out. However, if the payroll is not grouped by department, each individual employee must be considered. Any covered employees not being reported must be put on the audit report as findings. Proper units for these employees must be recorded. The auditor should also obtain the Social Security number, hire date and termination date for these employees, if applicable.

All new hires and terminations must be reviewed to verify timeliness of beginning and ending contributions. Any exceptions must be shown on the audit report.

If the employer is not reporting units correctly, this should be put on the audit report as well. What if an employer mistakenly omitted a week, or failed to report vacations? An efficient way to test for this is to take a sample of the employees reported and look at them for each week in a year. Using the employer's payroll calendar, the auditor can test an employer and determine if all pay periods are reported and all required units are reported. If this sample proves that required units are not being reported correctly, then the auditor can expand this to capture 100% of that particular error.

By identifying these errors and recording them electronically, the auditor can begin building the audit report while in the field. This is the manipulation of data discussed in Chapter 12.

It is also in the field where the auditor should draft a narrative of the audit. This includes the explanation of the employer's payroll and reporting system. It should also contain anything relevant to the audit findings. By doing this in the field, the auditor will be able to have any questions answered by the employer and ensure that he or she correctly documented the employer's procedures.

Tips for Payroll Auditors

Have all questions answered before leaving the field. This avoids delays in the office when finalizing the audit.

Preparing the Audit Report in the Office

Once back in the office, the auditor can continue with and finish the audit report. In some cases, the auditor will only have to print the report because it was completed in the field. Other times there may be more work involved. The auditor may work on producing the audit report or there may be instances where someone other than the auditor, such as a clerical person, works on the report. It depends on how the information was provided in the field or how the auditor documented findings during field work.

If the auditor has recorded and documented findings on a laptop in the field and now must manipulate the data onto the report, it makes sense for the auditor to complete the report. However, in a case where the employer gave the auditor a hard copy of payroll showing the misreported units, it may be more economical for a clerical person to enter that information onto the report rather than the auditor. This will free the auditor's time to complete other reports and save money for the plan due to the lower billing rate for the clerical person.

At this point, the auditor can also make any followup calls with the employer. Any questions regarding the information the auditor has obtained from the employer should be answered. One important item to remember: This is not the time to request new information from the employer because doing so will most likely hold up the audit.

The auditor should have a deadline as to when the audit report should be completed and turned in to his or her supervisor for review. Whether the deadline is from the plan or the payroll auditing firm, it is still necessary. The deadline ensures that the auditor stays current with the audit and doesn't put it aside because it is complex, time-consuming or missing information. The payroll audit manager can monitor deadlines and ensure the plan receives its completed audits in a timely manner.

Contents of the Audit Report

Certain information should be contained in the audit report. How it is presented should be in accordance with the agreement between the plan and the payroll auditor and therefore is not part of this discussion.

Certain information concerning the employer should be included in the audit report. This information includes the:

1. Employer's name, address, phone and fax numbers
2. Name and e-mail address of the person the payroll auditor dealt with in the field
3. Account number assigned by the plan to the employer
4. Employer's federal tax identification number
5. Period audited and the date of the audit.

The audit report should also contain a summary of the CBA terms or participation agreement terms that directly relate to the audit. This is the basis of contributions, such as hours worked or hours paid. The report should state whether there is a probationary exclusion, which determines when contributions should begin. The report should also show what the units to be contributed are for: hours, days, weeks, etc., and whether the units are capped. The contribution rates should also be listed with the effective date range.

The report should also contain a full-page schedule detailing comments about the audit. These comments should give an overview of the audit and should also contain the following:

1. The availability and condition of the employer's payroll records
2. Comments on each type of finding discovered during the audit
3. Any assumptions made by the auditor
4. Any special circumstances that affected the audit
5. Anything unusual encountered by the auditor that the reader of the report should know
6. An explanation of how interest charged on any deficiencies was calculated
7. The cost of the audit, legal fees and/or liquidated damages if any of these are being charged to the employer as a result of the audit
8. Any recommendations made (for example, how to improve the employer's payroll system) by the payroll auditor.

An efficient way to include comments in an audit report is to produce a standard list of comments for the plan. The list can be included in the audit template, and the auditor can choose the appropriate comments and insert them into the report. For example, if the plan calls for contributions to begin on the date of hire, an error would be an employer failing to begin contributions at an employee's hire date. Therefore, a standard comment to be chosen from this list would be, "The employer failed to make contributions from a covered employee's date of hire." This will keep language the same for each audit for the plan. It also avoids typographical, spelling and grammatical errors. The example here is simple, but with a more complex situation this becomes a great timesaver.

The audit report should also contain totals and details of those totals. The audit total may be presented in different ways and may, depending on the plan, include interest, legal fees, liquidated damages and audit costs. The schedules that detail these totals are comprised of misreported units. These can also be presented in different ways.

Deficiencies

Schedules

Each year of the audit period should have its own schedule. On this schedule the auditor will detail misreported units by month by employee. Monthly totals of misreported units multiplied by the contribution rate should be totaled for the amount of deficiency for that year of the audit period. The same is done for each year of the audit. But what should be reported on these spreadsheets? Here are a few examples.

For the sake of simplicity, the term *units* is used. Units can be hours, days, weeks, months, wages or shifts. The audit spreadsheet can show only the units that were misreported for a given month for an employee. The cause of each deficiency is not shown on the audit report. Only totals are shown for each month. This method is often not acceptable because no details are made available to the employer that may want to dispute a portion of the deficiency.

Another way to detail units is by error type by employee by month. As discussed in Chapter 12, by effectively using the computer an auditor can identify the error types, such as omitting holidays or overtime and clerical errors. This enables the auditor to group total deficiencies by error type, and it makes it easier for an employer to review the audit spreadsheet. If an employer only disputes one error type noted on the audit, the plan can at least pursue collection on the error types that are *not* disputed.

Different error types can be assigned codes, which can be standardized for all of the plan's audits. For example, a column can be placed next to the column with the employees' names on the spreadsheet. In this column a letter is placed that corresponds to the appropriate error type. A "C" may be for a clerical error, and an "H" may be for omitting holidays. These codes can also appear on the total summary page. Using standard error codes may allow the plan to determine which area contains the most deficiencies.

Some plans require reporting of hours paid, while other plans may require reporting hours worked. Since payroll records are kept based on hours paid, plans that require reporting of hours paid are usually understandable and calculating deficiencies is normally a simple matter.

The plan that requires reporting hours worked usually makes payroll auditing much more difficult. In those plans, hours paid for vacation, holiday and sick pay are not reportable because they are not hours worked. Even if reporting is based on hours paid, the auditor must understand how to report overtime. Most plans require actual hours paid even if some of the hours are paid at time-and-a-half or double-time rates. Some plans require time-and-a-half hours be reported as 1.5 hours for each hour paid and double-time hours reported as two hours for each hour paid.

There may also be cases where both hours and wages are required. This will likely result in two separate schedules for each year, but this doesn't mean twice the work. An auditor with a good knowledge of Excel spreadsheets can easily produce both schedules.

In certain plans, the employee's job class status or local union affiliation may affect the contribution rate or waiting time for contributions to begin. The audit spreadsheet should include this information when required. This may mean a separate schedule for part-time employees and full-time

Tips for Payroll Auditors

If job status or class is required on your report, use the employer's codes on your report for identity purposes. This will cause less confusion when the employer reviews the report.

A Payroll Auditor's Story

"I performed a payroll audit that showed a large deficiency. The employer disagreed only with our finding that required reportable hours from the first day of hire. Since we summarized reporting errors by type, we were able to isolate those hours relating to the first day of employment. The employer paid the deficiency for all other error types and then the plan and the employer could deal solely with the remaining first-day-of-employment issue."

—Phil Vivirito

employees for each year of the audit period. It may entail subtotaling by the local union within each schedule for each year of the audit, or it may be as simple as an extra column on the spreadsheet.

Tips for Payroll Auditors

If the plan's interest changes are tied into the federal discount rate, have a hyperlink to the Web site in the audit program in order to stay updated.

Calculation of Amount Due

The amount due as a result of the payroll audit should also be included in the report as its own schedule. This can also be presented in various ways. What is included in the amount due depends on the plan's policy.

Total deficiencies need to be shown. They can be shown subtotaled by each year of the audit period, then totaled or subtotaled by error types. In each way, the total from each year's schedule must tie into the yearly subtotal. If showing the totals by error type, the auditor can present to the plan the amount due in each year of the audit period for every type of misreported unit. The coding system mentioned earlier can be used here. For example, the same notations appear here that were used on the audit spreadsheet. Now the totals are shown as "C" for clerical error and "H" for omitted holiday.

Interest, liquidated damages and audit costs may be on the audit report. It depends on the plan's policy. Whatever is required should be included with the total deficiencies. It's always a good idea to state the percentage of liquidated damages and the date through which the interest is calculated. These should be accompanied by comments on the report.

Delinquencies

So far, this chapter has discussed how audit findings and deficiencies should be shown on the audit report. There may also be instances where the employer is delinquent and this delinquency must be shown on the audit report. This will occur when contribution reports are submitted to the plan without payment. Whether the delinquency should be shown in the audit report is a decision each plan should make. No matter whether the delinquency is disclosed or not disclosed in the audit report, the auditor will still audit the units associated with the delinquency to determine if they have been reported correctly.

One advantage of including the delinquency amount in the audit report is that the amount of the delinquency can be included in determining interest due and/or liquidated damages.

If the plan decides not to include the delinquency in the totals of the audit report, the plan may decide to have the auditor identify the delinquency and comment on collection efforts in the audit comment section of the report.

Who Gets the Audit Report?

Now that the payroll auditor has finished the audit report, where should it go? The auditor needs to refer to the plan's policy. It may go to the plan administrator, who will present it to the board of trustees. The auditor may have to provide copies to the plan's collection attorney as well. In some cases, the

A Payroll Auditor's Story

"One of my colleagues did a payroll audit in Texas. The employer disputed the findings and eventually the plan sued. By the time the trial took place, my colleague no longer worked with us. I had to testify in court, but my colleague had done such an excellent job in performing the audit that the work papers spoke for themselves. The judge had little sympathy for the employer, and the plan collected the full amount of the deficiency and all additional legal and audit fees."

—*Larry Beebe*

plan's policy may state that the employer is to get a draft of the audit report in order to review it and bring forth any disputes with the audit findings.

The audit report should contain sufficient information that makes further explanation unnecessary. The payroll auditor should be able to explain and defend the report at the time it is written and at any time in the future.

Tips for Payroll Auditors

The auditor should write the report as if he or she must defend it in court a year later. Defending the report at a later time in court seldom occurs, but establishing such a standard will lead to the production of a superior product. That is good news for the payroll auditor and goods news for the plan.

Chapter 14

Alter Ego and Double-Breasted Companies

What are alter ego companies, and what concern do they have for the payroll auditor? Are double-breasted companies the same as alter ego companies?

Definitions

In an article in the 2004 edition of *Employee Benefit Issues: The Multiemployer Perspective,* J. David Sackman stated: "Alter ego means 'other self.' The concept of the alter ego is that two entities are really one and the same, so that the court will ignore the technical difference between them."

In a 1984 decision, The National Labor Relations Board (Walter Yoder & Sons, 270 NLRB 652 FA.6) stated:

> [A] double breasted operation is one in which a contractor operates two companies, one unionized and the other non-unionized. Depending on how the companies are structured and operated, each may be a separate corporation or else both may be so interrelated that they constitute a single employer or one may be the alter ego of the other. A collective bargaining agreement signed by one of the companies would not bind the other if each were a separate corporation, but would bind the other if both constituted a single employer and the employees of both companies constitute a single appropriate bargaining unit or the nonsignatory company is an alter ego of the signatory company.

To summarize the above, an employer can legitimately have double-breasted operations where one of the companies is bound by a collective bargaining agreement (CBA) and the other company is not bound. If it is determined that the two companies are so interrelated that the nonunion company is an alter ego of the union company, then the nonunion company may be found to have a reporting obligation under the CBA. This is a matter the attorneys and the courts may ultimately have to decide.

Role of the Payroll Auditor

Before the payroll audit starts, the payroll auditor may be informed by the plan's attorney that certain information has been gathered suggesting that an employer has double-breasted operations. The plan's attorney may ask the payroll auditor to:

1. Ask for the payroll records of the nonunion company to examine during the course of the payroll audit.
2. Gather information concerning the double-breasted operations in order for the attorney to determine whether the nonunion company is an alter ego to the union company.

When the payroll auditor asks to examine the payroll records of the nonunion company, the request will most often be refused. The employer, in refusing the request, usually will inform the payroll auditor that the two companies are not related and that its obligation as an employer is to provide records only for the union company. The refusal is expected, and the payroll auditor simply informs the plan attorney of that fact.

In some rare instances the employer may allow the auditor access to the payroll records of the nonunion company. The payroll auditor would extract the same information as is normally gathered in any payroll audit and would ultimately determine whether the employer has any reporting obligation under the CBA for the employees of the nonunion company.

Information to Gather

Some of the evidence regarding double-breasted companies will be gathered by the plan's attorney or by the plan itself. This includes evidence concerning common ownership and control; the economic and administrative dependency of the companies on one another; and whether certain corporate formalities are maintained by and between the entities.

Other evidence can be gathered as part of the payroll audit. One method of gathering this information is to fill out the questionnaire in Appendix M. This questionnaire will require asking the employer many questions. The employer may cooperate and answer the questions of the payroll auditor, or the employer may refuse to provide any information concerning the nonunion entity.

The following is a listing of information that the payroll auditor will attempt to gather regarding double-breasted operations:

1. The names and titles of officers, shareholders and directors. Are the names and titles the same or are they different?
2. The name(s) of persons handling labor relations
3. The names of major customers
4. The types of businesses conducted by the two entities. Are they identical or are there differences?
5. The names of persons performing clerical, administrative, accounting, engineering, managerial and estimating services
6. Employees shared by both companies
7. Equipment shared by both companies. Often the payroll auditor does his or her work in an office next to the shop or yard maintained by the employer. This may present an opportunity to observe the company name on the supplies and/or equipment. Is the name on the equipment the name of the union company, the nonunion company or a mixture of both company names?
8. Do the two companies share contractor's licenses, bank accounts, general ledgers and other accounting records, insurance policies and tax returns?
9. What is the length of time that each company has been in business?
10. Telephone numbers. Often the payroll auditor may hear the telephone being answered by the employer when audit field work is conducted. Are the phones being answered in the name of the union company, the nonunion

company or both? Do the companies share the same telephone number?

In many instances, the payroll auditor may not be able to obtain much of the information in the above list. Whatever information the payroll auditor is able to gather should be documented accurately and thoroughly as soon as the field work on the audit is completed. The plan's attorney may ask the payroll auditor to document all that he or she noticed concerning the operations of both companies.

In concluding this discussion, it should be stressed that an employer can legitimately have double-breasted operations. It is only in those situations where one company is thought to be or found to be the alter ego of another company that the information gathered by the payroll auditor may prove to be critical.

Tips for Payroll Auditors

In auditing the payroll records of the union company, the payroll auditor may notice that some employees have a number of gaps in service during the year being audited. If so, ask if those employees were working for the nonunion companies during those gap periods.

Chapter 15

Collecting and Preventing Delinquent Employer Contributions

The best way of dealing with delinquent employer contributions is never to have any to begin with. Unfortunately, almost every employee benefit plan experiences delinquent employer contributions. Causes of delinquencies are too numerous to mention, as are the excuses offered by employers for the failure to pay the collectively bargained benefits. What can the plan do to minimize the collection problems with delinquent employers?

Establishing a Strong Collection Policy

Many employee benefit plans have written collection policies that are adopted by the trustees and are used to set guidelines for the administrator, plan attorneys, the trustees themselves and any other parties involved in the collection of employer contributions.

The topics covered by the collection policy may include:

- An overall policy detailing how the plan collects employer contributions
- The plan's rights under the Employee Retirement Income Security Act (ERISA) and other laws and regulations to enforce collections and to audit the payroll of contributing employers
- The due date of employer contributions and explanation of when employer contributions become delinquent
- The specific steps the plan expects to perform in collecting employer contributions
- The specifics of how the plan handles both underpayments and overpayments of employer contributions
- Detail as to how interest and liquidated damages are calculated as assessed
- A determination of when legal fees and audit fees are assessed
- The legal steps the plan will take once administrative steps are exhausted in enforcing the collection of delinquencies
- The employer's appeal rights in the collection process.

An example of a written collection policy is shown in Appendix A.

Establishing a Collection Committee

If collection of employer contributions is a major issue for a benefit plan, then the

Tips for Trustees

Expenses of the collection committee and expenses of the board of trustees are ordinary and necessary expenses of operating a plan. A plan could have labor and management negotiate an amount per hour, in the collective bargaining agreement (CBA), which would be used to cover the expenses of the collection committee. One plan has negotiated 5¢ per hour, which is given to the collection committee. One advantage of such a policy is that it puts everyone on notice that the plan takes its collection responsibilities seriously.

---

board of trustees should establish a collection committee. The collection committee should operate as a subcommittee of the board of trustees. There should be equal numbers of labor and management trustees. The meetings of the committee should be separate from the board of trustees meetings.

In addition to the trustees who are members of the collection committee, the attendees at the meetings should include the plan administrator, the employees of the plan responsible for collections, the auditor who performs the payroll audits and the plan attorney who is in charge of collections.

The primary functions of the committee are

1. Establish and maintain the plan's collection policy.
2. Hire the auditor who will perform the payroll audits.
3. Decide how often to routinely audit each contributing employer.
4. Decide when to conduct special audits based on complaints and/or items noted by the plan administrator.
5. Review and approve the audits submitted by the payroll auditor.
6. Send the audit reports to delinquent employers with a demand for payment.
7. Monitor plan delinquencies.
8. Hear any employer appeals and make recommendations to the board of trustees regarding final action.
9. Discuss methodologies of improving the collection progress and make recommendations to the board of trustees.

Stamp System

In most employee benefit plans, the contributing employer fills out a remittance report listing the names and Social Security numbers of those covered employees who worked during the reporting period and records the units (for example, hours paid) and/or wages paid for those employees. The employer completes the amount due to the plan by multiplying the units or wages paid by the rate specified in the CBA. The total amount due is calculated by adding the amounts due for all covered employees, and a check is sent to the plan for the calculated total.

The major problem is that the funds are received after the work has been performed. This gives the employer an opportunity not to remit on a timely basis or not to remit at all.

In some industries, particularly those where delinquencies are high, one way to prevent delinquencies is to employ a stamp system. In a stamp system, employers are required to prepay their employer contributions by purchasing stamps from the benefit plan. The stamps are elaborately designed, hard to duplicate and printed by firms specializing in their design. The stamps are prenumbered and are multipart. They come in various dominations, such as $1 stamps, $5 stamps and $20 stamps. The employer purchases, in advance, enough stamps to cover its obligations to the employee benefit plan (or plans). At the conclusion of a pay period, the employer passes one copy of the stamps to each covered employee to cover his or her benefits.

For example, John Jones works 40 hours and should receive $1.60 in pension contributions. He gets $64 in stamps which he pastes into a stamp book. The employer attaches the other part of the stamps for John Jones to the remittance report. When the plan gets the remittance reports, the stamps are scanned. Later when John Jones turns in his stamp book, his stamps are matched by the prenumbering system to the scanning from the remittance reports, and appropriate credit is given in the pension fund records. The plan gets its money in advance and the plan participants know that they have received appropriate credit because the stamps passed through their hands. Employees cannot sell or barter stamps because the employer has informed the plan which stamps have gone to a given individual.

The major disadvantages of the stamp system are the time involved and the costs of administration. Using remittance reports is simple and less costly (initially) than using a stamp system. The major advantages to the stamp system are that funds are collected in advance of the work being performed. The stamp system also discourages underreporting by the employer because the employee gets stamps for every reporting period and is likely to complain if the stamps are withheld.

Other Methods of Dealing With Delinquencies

There are some other ways the plan can deal with delinquent employers. One is to have the employer bonded. A surety bond in which a third party ensures that the employer will make payments to the plan is an option. Bonds are common in the construction industry. In this case the bond would be considered a performance and payment contract bond.

If an employer is working on a public works project or a federal government construction contract, the Davis-Bacon Act requires the employer to pay prevailing wages. Usually the employer has a certified payroll requirement with the Department of Labor (DOL). This payroll must list job classifications. The plan can request copies of the certified payroll, and it can be reviewed to ensure that all covered employees are being reported.

The plan can also track delinquencies one month past due and immediately send the employer a notice of delinquency. It can demand payment plus interest and liquidated damages. The plan can also threaten to assess any legal fees. If a plan strictly enforces this procedure, delinquencies should decrease. In the event of a habitual delinquent employer, the plan can audit the employer as well. It may even schedule a yearly audit for this employer.

If for some reason a certain geographical area or local union jurisdiction has a high amount of delinquent employers, the plan may choose to concentrate payroll audits in that particular area.

Chapter 16

The Future of Payroll Auditing

Payroll auditing has changed dramatically in the past 25 years. Improved technology in the office environment allows the payroll auditor of the present to do more work in a shorter time period. The auditor of the past had to haul bulky files to the site of the payroll audit and perform all of his or her work using a pencil and an adding machine or calculator. The laptop computer has eliminated most of the paper, and has almost eliminated the pencil and the adding machine or calculator. Fax machines, e-mail and voice mail have all had their roles in achieving time savings in a payroll audit.

Has change gone as far as it is going to go in saving time performing payroll audits, or are there still ways in which the payroll auditor of the future will save time and money? The authors are confident that technology advances in the future will result in the achievement of even more time savings in a payroll audit. By the time a future edition of this book comes off the press, a great deal of what is mentioned in this chapter will already be standard operating procedure in most payroll audits. Some payroll auditors may already be utilizing some of what is discussed in this chapter.

The following are a few areas where there should be significant time and dollar savings in producing payroll audits.

Technology

The auditor of the past used to carry listings of remittance reports into the field. Additional listings might break down the remittances alphabetically or by Social Security number. Now, all of that material is likely to be on the payroll auditor's laptop. The auditor of the future will have the complete files of the plan (and also the union sponsoring the plan) on the laptop or have a computer chip with satellite access, which allows instantaneous access to those records.

The plan of the future may specify that contributing employers use a specific program or a specific payroll service company to process the payroll. The payroll might then be scanned and sent directly to the payroll auditor. This may allow the auditor to avoid traveling to the employer to perform the payroll audit. The payroll auditor of the future may not even have to come into the office to accomplish the audit. The auditor might perform the audit from a remote location or while on vacation from a resort or a cruise ship.

The computer of the future may respond to the auditor's voice. Files and records might be called up quickly, and the comparison could be made between the remittance reports filed and the employer's payroll records as fast as the auditor can speak.

The payroll auditor now can have e-mail access to the plan, the payroll audit supervisor and the plan's collection attorney. If no one is there to respond to the e-mail, the auditor may have to wait for hours to get a question answered. In the future, everyone should have their computer with them, in one form or another, and access should be immediate. The auditor will get his or her question(s) answered promptly and research should be just as easy.

Electronic Data

In the future, the paperless environment should extend to filing remittance reports. Remittance reports will be filed online. Payments will be transmitted electronically. The payroll auditor may have a computer program tied to the plan's computer that will monitor the reporting by the employers and flag reports based on certain preset criteria. For example, the program may flag any employer whose remittance is $2,500 or more below the previous month's, or the auditor may receive a report showing all employers with remittances of $5,000 or more in the previous month that have not filed in the current month. The payroll auditor and/or the plan office, after appropriate research and resolution, may decide to audit a given employer or employers sooner than the normal audit sequence based upon the pattern of filing(s).

When the employer adds and deletes employees utilizing the current reporting system, mistakes are bound to happen. Names are not spelled properly. First and last names are transposed. Social Security numbers are transposed or recorded improperly. Social Security numbers are assigned to the wrong people. An electronic environment does not prevent these types of errors from occurring, but it makes them much less likely. Once recorded properly in the employer's payroll system, an electronic transfer of data should be error free.

Strengthening the Collection Process

One goal of payroll auditing is to help ensure that the collection system employed by the plan is operating as efficiently as possible. A paperless environment for the collection process will help. More sophisticated collection processes, such as an electronic stamp system, will also help. In the future, everyone should have a personal computer. Participants will be able to check regularly to verify that the proper contributions for employee benefits have been made on their behalf.

Unfortunately, as the collection process becomes more sophisticated, methods of avoiding the payment of contributions due will become more sophisticated as well. Auditors will have to be even savvier from a technological point of view.

How far will this evolutionary process go? Who knows, but it should be an interesting adventure for all of those involved.

Chapter 17

Frequently Asked Questions in Payroll Auditing

The following are questions frequently asked by employers, trustees and payroll auditors. In each category, the authors have asked the question and then given an appropriate response.

Employers' Questions

1. ***I only want to give you payroll records for collectively bargained employees. I don't want to give you records for office staff or officers of the company. Why is that a problem?***

The Supreme Court ruled, in the case of *Central States Southeast and Southwest Area Pension Fund v. Central Transport, Inc.*, that an employer must produce payroll records of all employees for the payroll auditor. The payroll auditor does not have any interest in the payroll records of noncollectively bargained employees. However, the payroll auditor must look at all payroll records in order to judge for himself or herself who the collectively bargained employees are. The auditor must gain independent assurance that he or she has examined all of the records of collectively bargained employees. On occasion, the employer may ask the auditor to sign a statement that the wages of noncollectively bargained employees will not be revealed to the plan. Under normal circumstances, the payroll auditor will probably agree to sign this statement. In some instances, the employer objects to showing individual salaries for officers and office employees. In this case, the payroll auditor may give the employer permission to blank out individual salaries and leave in the total so that overall payroll may be verified.

2. ***Why should I have to pay on nonunion employees? They cannot get benefits.***

The employer is not correct. The plan cannot discriminate in favor of a participant just because that participant is a union member. If a person's job is covered by the collective bargaining agreement (CBA), the employer must pay for that individual. Once the individual earns enough credits, he or she gets the benefits.

3. ***Our state is a right-to-work state. Why should I pay on those who choose not to join the union?***

Employees in a right-to-work state have the right to decide whether to join the union. Whether they join the union or not has nothing to do with their benefits. If they are performing work covered by the CBA, they must be contributed for.

4. ***Why should I pay on temporary employees or summer help? They will never receive a pension.***

Defined benefit plans recognize that not all employees who are contributed for will receive enough credit to earn a pension. In determining the pension benefits that participants will receive, the actuary takes into account that the pension fund will have the benefit of contributions made for some individuals even though a pension will never be paid to those individuals.

5. ***Why should I let you see my cash disbursements journal? That is a private record.***

The agreement and declaration of trust of the plan, which is signed by the employer, specifies that the plan is authorized to conduct a payroll audit and details the records that the payroll auditor will be entitled to examine during the audit. Normally, the agreement and declaration of trust specify that payroll records and cash disbursements journals may be examined. Some plans even include the general ledger and the income tax returns as records that may be examined in a payroll audit.

6. ***Why did the union select me for an audit?***

The payroll auditor should be quick to point out that the union had nothing to do with having the employer selected for the audit. The plan determines who will be audited, and the plan is managed by equal numbers of labor and management trustees.

There are many different reasons why the employer was selected for the payroll audit. The selection process may have been at random, where all employers had an equal chance of being selected for audit. The selection may have been as a result of complaints being filed by a participant; or it may have been as a result of something a plan employee noticed during the processing of remittance reports; or the plan may have a policy of auditing all employers on a four-year cycle, and the selected employer's number just came up. Most often, the auditor has nothing to do with the selection process and can honestly respond that he or she does not know why the employer was selected.

7. ***Why are you auditing me? I am sure you do not audit the employer trustees.***

The answer to this question, for most plans, is that the plan has a payroll audit program that calls for all employers, including companies owned by employer trustees, to be audited every three or four years. The employer trustees often insist that their companies be audited first to avoid any hint of favoritism or special treatment.

The payroll audit is not being performed to harass the employer, but rather to ensure the employer is reporting correctly and to determine that all covered employees receive the benefits to which they are entitled.

8. ***Why have you written down the hours paid for that employee? It says on his payroll record that he is a shop employee, and shop employees are not covered.***

Normally, shop employees (or other types of noncovered employees) are easily identified because their hourly rate of pay is lower and/or dissimilar to the wage rate of a covered employee. When the wage rate approximates the wage rates of covered employees, the payroll auditor writes down the hours paid and then does further research to determine if the individual is a covered employee.

9. ***Even though I am an owner of the business, I still spend a majority of my time working with the tools of the trade. Can't I be a covered employee?***

There are certain circumstances where owner/employees can be considered covered employees. Most plans allowing owner/employees to be reported detail the specific circumstances where they can be considered covered employees. The owner/employee normally must sign an agreement to be placed in this category.

10. ***Why should I pay for coverage for my son?***

Unless the son has an ownership interest in the company, he would be treated the same as any other covered employee.

11. ***I have been overpaying for years. Why can't I receive a refund for the entire amount of the overpayment?***

Many employee benefit plans specify that when an employer has overpaid contributions to the plan, the employer can receive a refund of no more than one year's overpayment to the plan.

12. ***Why do I have to pay on probationary employees?***

Probation to join the union or to attain seniority may be different from the probationary period needed before a person becomes a plan participant.

The CBA or participation agreement normally indicates whether contributions are due from the first day of employment, or whether there is a probationary period (e.g., 30 days or 60 days) before contributions are required. The payroll auditor should inform the employer that the CBA will be followed in determining the hours that should have been reported for probationary employees.

13. ***How long will the audit take?***

The payroll auditor should inform the employer, if asked, whether the audit is budgeted for a half day, a full day or multiple days. The payroll auditor should also tell the employer that the actual time will depend on such factors as the auditability of the records and the volume of records that must be examined. As the audit progresses, the auditor may inform the employer as to his or her progress and give a revised estimate of when the audit field work will be completed.

14. ***The local union's plan audited us last year. Why is the national plan auditing us this year?***

In an ideal world, all of the payroll audits for an employer could be done at the same time. Often it is difficult to coordinate the audits, and each plan must audit the employer when it can. The hours to be reported may not even be the same for both plans; therefore, the auditor may be looking at different records for a different time period. Also, the employer may be working in more than one local, and the local that audited last year may not be the same one that is affiliated with the national plan.

15. ***I am too busy to sit with the auditor all day. Do I have to?***

No. If the records are set aside for the audit, the employer (or its representative) often needs to spend very little time with the auditor. The employer normally only has to spend time at the very beginning to explain the records, be available to answer questions as the job progresses and be available at the conclusion for an exit interview. Most often the actual time spent with the payroll auditor is less than one hour.

16. ***The local union could not provide any workers when I needed them. Why should I contribute for workers that I hired without the local's help?***

The payroll auditor should tell the employer that the reporting obligation is for all individuals covered by the CBA, regardless of how they were obtained. The employer may have a legitimate complaint for the union to address, but it does not affect the plan's reporting requirements.

17. ***Why do I have to pay for vacation hours paid when an employee terminates?***

The CBA normally states that the employer is required to report all hours paid to covered employees. Vacation hours, whether paid before or after an employee terminates, are hours paid and must be reported.

18. ***I am a contractor in the construction industry. Why do I have to report on an employee if the person only worked for two weeks?***

In the construction industry, employees may change jobs frequently. The employee may only have worked for this particular employer for two weeks, but many have worked for other employers on a full-time basis. Proper reporting by each employer will ensure the individual gets the credit necessary to earn benefits under the plan.

Trustees' Questions

1. ***Why does the audit take so much time?***

Trustees don't often appreciate the amount of time required to do a proper payroll audit. The field work time on the audit may only be a day or even half a day. Once the payroll auditor leaves the field, there is a great deal of time involved in determining whether the employees who have not been reported should have been reported. Once that determination has been made, the unreported hours must be summarized and totaled by type of error. Then the audit report must be written.

There are many reasons why field work may take longer than necessary when the employer is in a remote location. The employer's records may not be in good order. The employer may not be prepared which keeps the payroll auditor waiting. The employer's records may not be conducive to an audit (e.g., they may be in employee number order). There may be numerous audit findings that require the auditor to look at 100% of the records.

2. ***How much should a payroll audit cost the plan?***

The cost of the payroll audit depends on the answers to many questions. Just a few of these questions are:

- Who is performing the payroll audit? Is it an internal audit staff or a CPA firm?
- Will the auditors look at all hours paid, or will they utilize a sampling approach?
- How large is the company being audited?
- Do the covered employees at the company represent a small or a large percentage of the workforce?
- Will the payroll auditor find a small or large number of errors?
- Will the employer have all records available and displayed in a logical sequence when the payroll audit starts?
- Does the payroll auditor have to measure hours paid, hours worked or some other unit?
- Are the hours paid weekly summarized by the month, by the quarter or annually?

A Payroll Auditor's Story

"An owner noted that I had recorded hours that had not been remitted for one employee. He said, 'I am not paying for him. He stole my truck.' I had to inform the employer that I was obligated to pick up all hours paid for all employees covered by the CBA."

—Tom Seay

3. ***Why don't we audit every employer every three years?***

The plan should measure annually the relationship between the funds collected as a result of the payroll audit program, and the cost of the audits. The goal is to collect more money performing payroll audits than the payroll audit program costs. Many successful payroll audit programs identify deficiencies that represent a multiple of the cost of the program. The amount of the multiple depends on such factors as the industry serviced by the plan and how rapidly the plan is able to identify and collect delinquencies.

The ideal time period to have an average employer in the plan may be three years—Or it could be four, five or six years. Each plan is different. Any given employer may be audited more or less frequently than every three years depending on the plan's history with that employer.

4. ***Should we have payroll auditors perform a 100% examination when an employer's payroll records are examined? Or should we instruct the auditor to sample the employer's payroll, isolate errors by type and then do a 100% examination on those error types?***

Some plans prefer the 100% audit. The major advantage of the 100% examination is that there is little likelihood that all errors will not be identified. The major disadvantage of this method is the cost. A 100% examination is extremely time-consuming. It works best when the plan has its own internal payroll audit staff. The majority of plans who do payroll audits do not perform a 100% examination.

5. ***Why can't the employer send us all the records to do a payroll audit in the payroll auditor's office?***

In the future, in a pure paperless environment, it may be possible to have all of the records forwarded to do an office audit. Until that time occurs, most payroll audits must be done in the employer's office. The sheer volume of records that must be reviewed necessitates that the payroll audit be done on site at the employer.

One other reason for doing the audit on site at the employer is that the payroll auditor has the opportunity to see how the employer operates. The auditor quickly discovers how cooperative the employer will be and almost as quickly determines whether deficiencies are likely to be found in the audit.

Payroll Auditors' Questions

1. ***What should I do if I show up for a payroll audit and find no one at the employer's premises?***

After checking his or her own records to ensure he or she is at the right place at the right time and date, the payroll auditor should immediately call the employer's phone number. If it is possible to send an e-mail to the employer, this should also be tried. If there is no response after a reasonable time period (one-half hour to an hour), the payroll auditor should leave a note stating the facts and circumstances. If the plan's agreement and declaration of trust states that audit cost will be assessed if an employer cancels at the last minute or does not show up, that fact should be included in the note. The employer should then be referred to the plan itself or the plan attorney for rescheduling.

2. ***What should I do if a key employee (e.g., the bookkeeper who handles the payroll records) is a no-show? Or if the employer cancels at the last minute, or when the payroll auditor arrives to conduct the audit?***

Ask the employer if anyone else in the company can provide you with the information to do the audit, or ask if the records have already been gathered for you. If the answer is *no,* the employer should be shown the section of the agreement and the declaration of trust that permits the plan to charge audit costs if the payroll audit is delayed or canceled. The employer should also be provided with a copy of the note the payroll auditor will submit to the plan explaining why the payroll audit could not be conducted.

3. ***What should I do if I finish the field work of the payroll audit ahead of schedule?***

Under these circumstances, the payroll auditor has several choices:

- Stay at the employer and write the report. The audit report is produced when the facts and circumstances of the audit are best remembered. This choice may not be possible if additional information is needed from the plan to finish the audit.
- Go back to the hotel if out of town and there are other audits scheduled in that area during the week, or go back to the office if in town.
- Call the next employer to be audited and start the field work on that job. To do this, the employers should be advised in advance that although they are scheduled for a given time on a certain date, circumstances may change and the auditor may call them and want to arrive early. Most employers are very understanding and accommodating to this request.

4. ***If I am not done with the audit, after a full day's work, and I found no deficiencies or only a small number of deficiencies, should I go back to the employer for a second day of field work?***

Normally the answer should be *no.* Only in rare circumstances does going back the second day prove to be worthwhile. If the auditor is in doubt, he or she should call the payroll audit supervisor and discuss the situation. During the course of that conversation, the two parties can often agree whether to go back or to wrap up the audit. Most often, when the auditor is in doubt it is not worthwhile to come back for another day.

5. ***During the course of the payroll audit, I found a certain group of employees and am unsure if they are collectively bargained employees. What should I do?***

If the payroll auditor is still unsure after discussing the situation with the employer, calling the payroll audit supervisor and/or calling the plan's employee who deals with delinquencies, the hours and/or wages for these employees should be recorded and further research should be done back at the office or the plan. As one seasoned plan administrator said, "When in doubt, pick them up." If the auditor is still in doubt when the report is written, "When in doubt, include them in the report." The plan's representative can always exclude the hours/wages if evidence is shown that the employees should not be included. An audit report is not final until the payroll audit administrator says that it is. A list of these employees can

Tips for Payroll Auditors

Sometimes when the employer is a no-show, the auditor can leave the premises and get a cup of coffee, then show up again an hour later. It is amazing how often the employer has shown up in the interval.

also be left with the employer, for him or her to provide evidence as to why they are not covered employees.

6. ***If an employer utilizes many trades, only a small portion of the employees may be covered by the plan I am auditing. What should I do if the employer's payroll records do not adequately show the job classifications of its employees, making it difficult or impossible for me to perform the audit?***

Often, the payroll auditor makes a statement as to the adequacy of the employer's payroll records. This may be one of those situations where the auditor states that the employer's payroll records are not adequate for reporting purposes. The plan (and/or the plan's attorney) would then determine the appropriate action to take.

7. ***The employer has gone out of business. When I called to perform the final audit, I was informed that the records are unavailable because they are in storage. What should I do?***

If the records are in storage, it does not mean that they are unavailable. The auditor, or if necessary the plan attorney, should advise the employer that an obligation exists, under the agreement and declaration of trust, to produce the records. The auditor should be precise in stating exactly what records the employer needs to produce. In some instances, the auditor may go with the employer to the storage location to retrieve the necessary records. The audit can then be performed where office space can be found. Sometimes this means that the payroll auditor takes the records back to his or her office.

The auditor may not be able to find all of the employer's records. If one year or part of a year is missing, audit findings may need to be extrapolated for that period. Sometimes Forms W-2 can be obtained from IRS. It may also be possible for the employer's payroll processor to reproduce the missing records.

8. ***How should I deal with a verbally abusive employer? Or with an employer that threatens? Or with an employer that curses constantly?***

The first thing the payroll auditor should remember is to remain professional at all times. A payroll auditor should not tolerate any of these situations. He or she should tell the employer that the behavior is offensive and, if continued, will result in a suspension of the audit. If the employer persists, then the payroll auditor should leave the premises. The payroll auditor should immediately record everything the employer said and did and should then call the plan administrator. Normally the plan administrator will forward this to the plan attorney, who will make arrangements for the audit to be continued in an environment where the auditor does not have to interact with the abusive employer.

9. ***What should I do if the employer refuses access to the records of leased individuals because they are not employed by the company?***

The payroll auditor should inform the employer that the agreement it signed requires reporting of all individuals working in job classifications covered by the CBA. Inform the employer that unless these records are provided, the auditor will assume that all payments to temporary agencies for leased employees are for covered employment. In many instances the employer will still resist, and this matter may have to be referred to the plan's attorney for resolution.

10. ***During field work, I noticed that more than one company appears to be operating from the same premises. What should I do?***

The payroll auditor should tell the

employer about his or her observation and ask what the other company does. The employer may state that the other company has nothing to do with employment under the CBA and may offer proof regarding this statement. If the auditor is satisfied with the employer's explanation, he or she would normally take no further action other than notifying the plan as to his or her observation.

The employer may say that it is none of the payroll auditor's business what the other company does, or may say, "That is our nonunion company." In those instances, the auditor should refer to Chapter 14 in this book (Alter Ego and Double-Breasted Companies) and gather as much information as possible while in the field regarding these related companies. This information can then be forwarded to the plan for appropriate action.

11. ***What should I do if the employer states that I have to be finished by 3:30 because that is closing time, or says that I only have five hours to do the audit?***

The payroll auditor should politely state to the employer that the payroll audit will be performed as quickly as possible, but that the auditor, and the auditor alone, decides when the field work on the audit is finished. Tell the employer that if the audit is not completed today, the auditor will come back tomorrow or at a mutually agreeable time and date. If the employer refuses to cooperate, refer the matter to the plan for appropriate action. What the auditor cannot do is let the employer fix the length of time for the audit.

12. ***The employer representative says that he or she has to leave at 4:00, but that I am welcome to stay to finish the audit. What should I do?***

This is a decision for the auditor to make. The auditor may feel comfortable staying, particularly where other employees may still be working in the office. Or, he or she may not be comfortable, particularly if no one else will be in the office. The auditor may have to schedule another day and time to complete the audit, particularly if an exit interview must be conducted. One solution may be to ask the employer if the auditor can take certain records back to the office (or to the hotel) to complete the audit. The records can then be returned the following day. Often the employer will allow the records to be removed only if the auditor promises not to copy them and to return them intact.

13. ***The employer has records that are incomplete. What should I do?***

It depends on what is missing. If the payroll records are complete for 75% of the audited period, then the audit can be completed for that portion of time and, depending on the findings, the employer can be compelled by fund counsel to produce the missing records. If the employer is unable or unwilling to produce payroll records for what it says are noncollectively bargained employees, then the auditor cannot complete the audit. Fund counsel should compel the employer to produce records for all employees for the entire period.

14. ***At the midpoint of the audit, the employer asks me to leave and turn over all the notes and working papers. What should I do?***

The auditor has no choice but to leave. The auditor should inform the employer that the working papers are his or her property and are not to be relinquished. If the employer becomes adversarial, then the auditor may have no choice but to leave the working papers with the employer. The auditor should then call fund counsel and tell the full story.

15. ***The employer states that some or all of the covered employers sometimes do noncovered work and are therefore not reported for those time periods. What should be done?***

Unless the employer can furnish proof that the employees are doing noncovered work and are paid at a rate different than the prevailing wage rate under the contract, then all hours must be treated as reportable.

A Payroll Auditor's Story

"Sometimes the way to get the audit done is to adjust to the employer's schedule. I had one employer tell me he would get there at 5:00 a.m. the next morning. He certainly was surprised when I met him in the dark parking lot the next day."

—Tom Seay

Chapter 18

Conclusion

Conducting an efficient payroll auditing program is not easy. Many decisions must be made and the process itself is ever-changing. There is no perfect way to conduct payroll audits. What works well for one plan may not work at all for another plan.

What the authors have tried to do in this book is to illustrate some of the best practices that they have seen in conducting payroll audits based upon their years of experience. The intent of this book is to be a supermarket of ideas, forms and checklists that can be used in the trustees' payroll audit program. In this supermarket, pick up what works and leave the remainder on the shelf.

The trustees may decide, in a given area, that their method works better than anything the authors have suggested. The trustees may not like the form or checklist included in this book because they have a better form or checklist. Use the method that works best.

This book is a work in progress. The authors want to publish a second edition of this book eventually. In order to make this second edition even better, the authors need the readers' help. Send thoughts and stories about payroll auditing. If we use your story on payroll auditing, we will attribute it to you. Send forms and checklists. The goal is to have an efficient payroll auditing program.

Larry Beebe and Phil Vivirito
Bond Beebe
4600 East-West Highway, Suite 900
Bethesda, MD 20814
(301) 272-6000
beebe@bbcpa.com or vivirito@bbcpa.com

Collection Policy

The Board of Trustees of the XYZ Plan hereby adopts the following policy for the collections.

Section 1: General Policy

It is the policy of the Plan to collect all employer contributions as they are due, and to make such diligent and systematic efforts as are appropriate under the circumstances to do so.

The Trustees have the legal right to exercise all remedies allowable under the Trust Agreements and under the Employee Retirement Income Security Act of 1974, as amended ("ERISA"), including but not limited to:

1. The right to establish a date on which contributions are due;
2. The right to audit the financial records of the employers, including but not limited to payroll ledgers, federal and state tax returns, IRS Form 941 and such other books and records of the employers that are necessary in order for the auditor to give an unqualified opinion that the proper contributions have been made;
3. The right to establish a random audit program;
4. The right to require that the delinquent employer pay the cost of an audit, interest, attorney fees, and any other expenses incurred by the Plan in determining the amount of a delinquency and in collecting the delinquency;
5. The right to recover liquidated damages;
6. The right to require a bond or a cash deposit as security for prompt future payments due from an employer that has been habitually delinquent in its contributions to the Plan; and
7. The right to take all other steps and to perform all other acts that are necessary in order to collect contributions due to the Plan in a timely and expeditious manner.

The procedures set forth herein shall be followed unless the Board of Trustees determines that they should be waived in a particular instance.

Section 2: Collection Procedure

In accordance with the Trust Agreement, ERISA and the above declaration of policy, the following administrative steps shall be taken to effectuate the collection of delinquent contributions.

1. To the extent practicable, in addition to the procedures described below, the administrative manager shall contact

the employer and the local union by telephone, to attempt to effectuate payment of contributions, in the event the Plan has not received contributions when due.

2. Contributions and the supporting remittance report (collectively referred to herein as "Contributions") are due on the date the employer's collective bargaining agreement requires payment; if the collective bargaining agreement does not state a due date, payment is due on the last day of the month following the month in which the work was performed for which the contributions are owed (either date to be referred to as the "Due Date").
3. If contributions are not received within five business days of the Due Date, the Plan's administrative manager shall send a first notice of delinquency to the employer requesting immediate payment. The notice shall advise the employer that the contributions must be sent immediately to avoid interest charges and liquidated damages.
4. If the delinquent Contributions are not received by the administrative manager within ten business days of the Due Date, the administrator shall immediately send a second notice. The notice shall state that the employer is liable for interest charges, liquidated damages, attorney fees and court costs incurred in the collection of the Contributions, as described in Section 5 hereof. The notice also shall advise that if payment is not received within five business days of the mailing of the second notice, the delinquency will be referred to the Plan's legal counsel for collection.
5. If the Contributions are not received within ten business days of the date of the second notice, the administrative manager shall refer the delinquency to legal counsel, with copies of the first and second notices.
6. Legal counsel shall follow the procedures set out in Section 3 of these Rules.
7. If an employer makes payment of the amount of the delinquency but not payment of accrued interest and other amounts owed, acceptance of the payment shall not constitute a waiver of the Plan's claim for such accrued interest and other amounts.
8. When an employer submits a report and payment that is significantly lower than its preceding report, the administrative manager shall seek to reconcile what appears to be a discrepancy by contacting the employer and the chief executive officer of the local union on the matter. If the apparent discrepancy is not explained, the administrative manager shall report the situation to the Board of Trustees at their next regularly scheduled meeting.
9. If an employer believes that it has overpaid contributions, the employer shall bring the matter to the attention of the administrative manager. If the administrative manager concludes that the employer has overpaid its contributions for a period of three months or less, a credit may be taken in the month following the administrative manager's determination, provided, however, that in no event shall a credit be taken or allowed where a premium has already been paid by the Plan to provide coverage for any benefits or benefits have already been provided at the time the purported overpayment is brought to the attention of the administrative manager. The administrative

manager shall refer any requests for credits for overpayments of contributions occurring during a period in excess of three months' duration to the Delinquency Committee. No interest credit shall be allowed to the employer on any overpayment.

Note: Other items that might be contained in a collection policy include:

1. The process whereby employers are selected for a payroll audit
2. The appeals process when amounts are assessed as a result of the payroll audit process
3. The establishment and duties of a collection committee
4. Details of how liquidated damages, audit costs and legal fees are assessed
5. How interest charged on delinquencies is calculated.

Engagement Letter

Date

Board of Trustees

Dear Members of the Board:

We are pleased to confirm our understanding of the services we will provide to the ______________________("Plan") in connection with the audits of employer payroll records.

The following enumerates the services the auditing firm will provide to the Plan:

I. Performance of Audits

The auditing firm will audit the books and records of the contributing employer as directed by the Plan's Board of Trustees and in accordance with the Plan's Policy for the Collection of Delinquent Contributions ("Policy"). The period that will be audited will be in accordance with the Policy and may also be at the discretion of the Board of Trustees.

The auditing firm will conduct each payroll audit in accordance with industry professional standards. Audit procedures generally will include completion by the auditing firm of the following:

1. Review of the applicable Collective Bargaining Agreement and Standard Form of Agreements and other relevant documents and data regarding contribution obligations to the Plan. Consultations with the Plan Office and the Local Union will occur as necessary.
2. Review of employee payroll records, including comparison of payroll records to government filed reports such as W-2 forms and Form 941.
3. Determination as to whether the calculation of contributions per employee has been properly included in contributions reports as submitted to the Plan. Depending upon the method of calculation, as well as the number of employees employed with a particular contributing employer, the auditing firm will decide whether this procedure can be done on a test basis, or on a complete basis in the absence of specific instructions from the Board of Trustees.
4. Issue status reports and other documents regarding audit progress, information on data received from the Plan, appointment schedule and completed audit date.

5. In the event that the contributing employer refuses access to applicable records, the auditing firm will take action as required under the Policy.
6. Upon the conclusion of field audits of the contributing employer, the auditing firm will conduct an exit interview with the contributing employer and prepare an inquiry letter, as necessary, regarding requests for information or clarification from the employer, identifying any unresolved issues. The auditing firm will prepare a written report for distribution to the Plan regarding the audit findings, including information about any delinquencies and/or overpayments.
7. In the event that expert testimony is needed regarding any of the payroll audits performed, the auditing firm will bill the Plan at the standard hourly rates for such testimony as provided in Section II. The auditing firm personnel will also be available to the Plan regarding general advice on the Plan's payroll audit program.

II. Payroll Audit Fees

Fees for the above-mentioned services will be based on the amount of time expended by each professional completing payroll audits at the standard hourly rate identified below.

Principal $ __________
Manager $ __________
Payroll Auditor $ __________

In the event that circumstances occur that would have a substantial impact on the scope of work to be performed, the auditing firm will notify the Plan to discuss these circumstances and request authorization before incurring additional time and expense.

Each audit of a contributing employer will be billed as a separate project subject. Invoices for services are rendered when the payroll audits are completed and written reports are forwarded to the Plan. Invoices are payable within 30 days of the invoice date.

III. Administrative Provisions

1. The auditing firm will maintain appropriate and adequate professional liability insurance during the period it is retained to provide services to the Plan. A copy of the auditing firm's most recent insurance certificate is to be provided upon request from the Plan.
2. The auditing firm agrees that it will not subcontract any work performed on behalf of the Plan under this engagement letter.
3. The Board of Trustees and the auditing firm can terminate this engagement letter upon 30 days advanced, written notice, with or without cause. Work pending as of the date notice of the termination is received will be completed under the terms set out above, unless other terms are specifically agreed to, in writing, by the parties. No new projects will be started after receipt of a termination notice. Upon expiration of the termination notice, the auditing firm will submit final invoices and transfer all required Plan information to the Plan or its designated agent. The auditing firm will cooperate with the Plan to provide for the expeditious transfer of the Plan's files and records to the person or entity designated in writing by the Plan.

4. It is agreed that the auditing firm shall not disclose information involving the Plan except as necessary to perform services under this engagement letter, and shall take all appropriate and reasonable measures to ensure and maintain confidentiality regarding all matters involving the Plan.
5. This engagement letter may be amended, as necessary, by the Plan or the auditing firm, in writing, and as signed by the Plan and the auditing firm.
6. The auditing firm shall indemnify, defend and hold harmless the Plan and its Trustees, employees, or agents from and against any and all claims, actions, demands, costs and expenses, including reasonable attorney fees and disbursements, as a result of a breach by the auditing firm of any of its obligations under this engagement letter or arising out of the negligent act, omission, willful misconduct, breach of any obligation or failure to comply with any applicable law or regulation or provision of this letter agreement by the auditing firm or any of its employees, agents or representatives.

   The Plan shall indemnify, defend and hold harmless the auditing firm, its officers, directors, employees and agents from and against any and all claims, actions, demands, costs and expenses, including reasonable attorney fees and disbursements, as a result of a breach by the Plan of any of their obligations under this engagement letter or arising out of the negligent act, omission, willful misconduct, breach of any obligation or failure to comply with any applicable law or regulation or provision of this letter agreement by the Plan or any of its Trustees, employees or agents.
7. The effective date of this engagement letter is the last date of the last signature as set forth below. This engagement letter will continue in effect for three years as of that date. This engagement letter will automatically renew annually as of the effective date unless otherwise terminated by the Plan or the auditing firm as provided in paragraph 3 above.
8. This engagement letter constitutes the entire understanding and agreement of the Plan and the auditing firm and supersedes all prior understandings between the parties relating to the services provided hereunder.

Very truly yours,
The Auditing Firm
By:______________________________
Auditor Representative

Acknowledged and Agreed to:
Board of Trustees
________________________Plan

____
Chairman

Date:________________________

____
Secretary

Letter to Employer Selected for a Payroll Audit

Date

Company
123 Street
Anywhere, USA
RE: Pension Plan for Company

The detailed basis on which you make contributions to the ____________ Pension Fund is set forth in the Standard Form of Agreement of Participation. Such Agreement for Participation also provides that the employer agrees to become a party to the Agreement and Declaration of Trust. Audits of employer payroll records as they relate to contribution to the Fund are authorized by Article ___, Section ____ of the Agreement and Declaration of Trust.

The Board of Trustees has adopted a program calling for periodic payroll audits of participating employers. This is to advise you that your company and other companies in your area will be audited in the very near future.

The Board of Trustees has retained the accounting firm of ____________________________ located in ______________________________ to conduct these routine compliance reviews. In the near future, you will be contacted by a representative of that firm to set an appointment to conduct a review of your firm's payroll records. Given the limited time that our auditors are in your area, I appreciate your efforts in accommodating their scheduling needs.

Sincerely,

Administrative Officer

Payroll Audit Program—Example 1

Client:______________________________
Employer:____________________________

This payroll audit program has been prepared to provide the payroll auditor an effective tool for planning compliance audit procedures and for supervising and controlling the performance of the compliance audit work. Development of a payroll audit program for each engagement will provide a historical record of the work done as well as information to be used in the report of the audit.

This payroll audit program is not designed to fit all payroll audit engagements. It should be revised whenever the auditor, in the course of the work, finds that changes and/or additions to the programmed procedures are necessary to complete the payroll audit. A thorough evaluation of the adequacy of the Employer's payroll records should be the starting point of a compliance audit. This review helps to determine the degree of reliability that may be placed on the payroll records, and in turn determines the nature and extent of the payroll auditing procedures to be used and the tests to be conducted during the compliance audit.

You are urged to read the payroll audit program in its entirety before performing any of the payroll audit procedures described in a particular section.

1. **Prior to Entering the Field**
   A. The purpose of the payroll audit is to determine if the employer is in compliance with the terms of the Collective Bargaining Agreement with regard to plans the employer is required to contribute to, and ascertain that the contribution reports are correct.

Auditor______________
Reviewer______________

B. Documents provided from Plan for the entire audit period requested:
   - Contribution reports ____________
   - Collective Bargaining Agreements ____________
   - Standard Form of Participation ____________
   - Accounts receivable ____________

C. Correspondence from Plan and/or Local Union:
   - Plan Contact letter ____________
   - Memo(s) ____________
   - Other correspondence ____________

D. Plans to be audited:

____

E. Payroll auditor's correspondence:
   - Confirmation letter mailed/faxed on ____________
   - Other ____________

2. **Field Work**

A. Audit period requested: ____________

Records we requested by our confirmation letter:
Payroll Registers, Individual Earnings Records, 941 Forms, U/C Forms, W2s, W3s, 1099s, 1096s, LM-2s, Contribution reports for all Plans contributed to, Personnel Files, I-9s, Cash Disbursement Journals

B. Are records available for the audit period? ____________

C. Explain what records are unavailable and why:

____

____

D. Explain what records are available for each year:

Year	Records
______	____________________________________
______	____________________________________
______	____________________________________

Auditor ____________
Reviewer ____________

E. Payroll reconciliation:
Quarter Selected: ______________

	Payroll	941	State Unemployment Tax Returns
Gross wages paid			
Adjustments			
Reconciled wages	$0.00	$0.00	$0.00

If unable to reconcile above, how was it determined that the complete payroll was made available?

F. Type of payroll: ____________________ Employee sort: ____________________
Pay types: ____________________
Cycle: ____________________ W/E date: ________ Pay date: ________
Covered Department: ____________________
Number of employees on payroll: ____________________
Approximate number of covered employees: ____________________
Other Plans or Unions: ____________________

G. Explanation of employers' accounting and reporting system:

H. Payroll auditing testing: *Scope of Test*

Bargaining Unit ____________________
Units ____________________
Holiday ____________________
Vacation ____________________
Hires ____________________
Terms ____________________
Pay Periods ____________________
Rates ____________________

Auditor ______________
Reviewer ______________

Additional Tests for 401(k) Plan

Starts ______

Stops ______

Employee pretax deferral ______

Employee after-tax deferral ______

Employer Match ______

Nonelected Contribution ______

Loan Payments ______

I. Results of Testing: *Results*

Bargaining Unit ______

Units ______

Holiday ______

Vacation ______

Hires ______

Terms ______

Pay Periods ______

Rates ______

Additional Results for 401(k) Plan

Starts ______

Stops ______

Employee pretax deferral ______

Employee after-tax deferral ______

Employer Match ______

Nonelected Contribution ______

Loan Payments ______

J. Does the employer use a temporary employment agency? ______
Does the employer have any individuals that are issued Form 1099s (if so, see attached)? ______

K. Has the company changed ownership during the audit period (if so, include documentation)? ______

L. Did the audit include any salaried employees (if so, specify who and on what basis)? ______

M. Are there any special instructions from the Plan which need to be addressed? If this is a target or priority audit, were all issues addressed?

______

______

Auditor ______

Reviewer ______

N. When does the employer submit contributions, employee and employer, and loan payments?

____

____

____

____

O. Did you obtain census information for all employees not reported? If not, explain why.

____

P. If requested, sample of employee birth dates (necessary for actuarial purposes):

Name	SSN	Birth Date

Q. List owners/officers if required:

Name	SSN	Title

R Conclude on payroll audit findings:

____

____

3. **Exit Interview**

A. Conduct an exit interview according to the Plan's policy.

B. Employer will be sent a: ____________________

C. Employer representative(s) present during exit interview:

Name	Title

D. Employer's response to exit interview:

____

____

____

____

Auditor ________________

Reviewer ________________

4. **Payroll Audit Report**

   A. List all exceptions. Provide explanation as to the nature of each exception. Include hire, termination and eligibility dates where applicable. Document rate changes. Provide employee class where applicable.

   B. Compute the amount of underpayment.

   C. Compute interest according to the Plan's policy.

5. **Submission of Completed Audit**

   Control sheet and audit program completed. Correct number of audit report copies enclosed. File saved to network correctly.

   Auditor: ______________________________

   Auditor Signature: ______________________________ Date: ____________

6. **File Review**

   Reviewer: ______________________________ Date: ____________

Auditor ____________

Reviewer ____________

Payroll Audit Program—Example 2

	Date Performed	Initials	W/P Reference
General			
1. Read the general information and suggested field audit program.	______	______	______
2. Obtain a copy of the CBA.	______	______	______
3. If appropriate, ask the questions in the attached Questions for Local Union Representative.	______	______	______
4. Read the CBA including the model clause to gain an understanding of the Plan and the Union.	______	______	______
5. Call the Plan or your company administrator with any questions.	______	______	______
6. Contact the Employer and schedule the payroll audit.	______	______	______
Initial Procedures			
1. Go over the list of items requested with the Employer or its representative to ensure that all items are available.	______	______	______
2. Gain an understanding of how the payroll system works—quickly.	______	______	______
3. Ask the Employer for a copy of the worksheets used to prepare the remittance reports.	______	______	______
4. Start with the prior year. Trace hours reported for one to three employees from the employee payroll records to the work sheets to the alpha listing of the remittance reports.	______	______	______

	Date Performed	Initials	W/P Reference
5. Using your judgment, select individual payroll records and determine if the following types of errors exist.			
a. Failure to report new employees			
b. Failure to report temporary employees			
c. Failure to report terminating employees			
d. Failure to report overtime hours paid			
e. Failure to report vacation hours paid			
f. Failure to report paid holiday hours			
g. Failure to contribute for apprentices			
h. Failure to report for covered nonunion employees			
i. Failure to report fractional hours paid			

Secondary Procedures

	Date Performed	Initials	W/P Reference
1. Isolate all error types and test extensively (100% if appropriate) to determine total deficiencies.			
2. Determine if there has been a change of bookkeepers during the audited period. Perform some tests on each bookkeeper's work if deemed necessary.			
3. Scan cash disbursements journal or checkbooks and Form 1099s for payments to subcontractors.			
4. Scan state quarterly unemployment returns to determine if you were given payroll records for all employees.			
5. If necessary, check quarterly payroll tax returns to the W-2s.			
6. If necessary, scan W-2s to determine if you were given payroll records for all employees.			
7. Spot-check timecards, if necessary, to employee's payroll records.			
8. Call the Plan office to run Social Security numbers of any employees you are unsure of (to be done before you have summarized hours for these employees).			
9. Note hours paid to all covered employees for months not remitted for by the Employer.			

	Date Performed	Initials	W/P Reference
Finishing Field Work			
1. Prepare a preliminary work paper noting the deficiencies found.	________	________	________
2. Prepare a work paper detailing items or hours still to be resolved.	________	________	________
3. Discuss both of the above work papers with the Employer. Note the Employer's comments.	________	________	________
4. Provide the Employer with a copy of your findings work paper.	________	________	________
5. Ask the Employer who the owners and officers of the business are.	________	________	________
6. Ask the Employer if there are any questions regarding proper reporting procedures to the Plan.	________	________	________
7. Compare remittance reports in Employer's possession to Plan records to determine that they all have been filed.	________	________	________
Followup and Report Writing			
1. Contact the Plan concerning questionable items.	________	________	________
2. Write a letter to the Employer, if necessary, to resolve any open items.	________	________	________
3. Contact local union business agent, if appropriate, concerning questionable items.	________	________	________
4. Resolve all items in doubt.	________	________	________
5. Write the report.	________	________	________
6. Calculate and insert, if necessary, the cost of the audit.	________	________	________
7. Calculate and insert interest on deficiencies.	________	________	________

Warning: Only under unusual circumstances should all of the procedures shown in this audit program be performed and/or documented. The purpose of the audit is to determine deficiencies. When deficiencies are found, then documentation of the facts and circumstances is essential.

Report of Independent Payroll Auditors

The Board of Trustees
Pension Plan

We have applied certain agreed-upon procedures, as set forth in our payroll audit program, to the accounting records of ABC Company (the Employer), Account Number 1234, to determine whether the Employer has accurately reported hours on behalf of the employees covered by the Collective Bargaining Agreement. This report is to be used solely to determine the accuracy of the remittance reports filed and contributions paid by the Employer for the period January 2003 through December 2005, and is not to be used for any other purpose.

No exceptions to the Employer contributions were noted.

Tips for Out-of-Town Payroll Audits

1. Have a letter of introduction.
2. Get good directions and find the employer the night before.
3. Learn as much as you can about the employer's payroll system before you arrive.
4. Make sure all materials you asked for are present when you arrive.
5. Have your own copies (or a summary) of remittance reports.
6. Get there as early in the morning as you can.
7. Don't spend your time proving that the totals of the payroll tax returns are accurate. Use them to identify unreported employees.
8. Look for deficiencies.
9. When you find a deficiency, expand your testing.
10. Scan cash disbursements journals for subcontract payments.
11. List names, Social Security numbers, and wages or hours for unreported employees.
12. Look for related "double-breasted" companies.
13. Don't waste time if you don't find deficiencies.
14. Leave the employer a list of information not provided.
15. Call the fund administrator or fund attorney to ask for advice.
16. When in doubt, write up the potential deficiency.
17. Use the computer to save time on the job.
18. Write your report at night in the hotel.

Letter From Auditor to Employer Regarding Upcoming Payroll Audit

Date

Contact
Company
Address
City, State, ZIP

RE: Payroll Audit for the Plan

Dear ____,

This letter will confirm our appointment to perform a payroll audit of __(company name)__ to the Plan on _(date and time)._ This audit will cover the period January 20xx through December 20xx.

In order to facilitate the audit, we will require that the following records and documents be made available:

1. Payroll records including detail on wages and hours worked and paid (weekly or monthly)
2. Individual employees' earnings records (quarterly or yearly)
3. Employer's Federal 941 Quarterly Payroll Tax Returns and Forms W-2, W-3, 1099 and 1096
4. Quarterly Unemployment Compensation Reports
5. Employer copies of monthly contribution reports to all fringe benefit funds to which you contribute
6. Cash disbursements records relevant to payroll
7. All pertinent personnel information, such as hire and termination dates.

Should you have any questions, ________________ can be reached directly at ____________ or via e-mail at __________________________. Thank you in advance for your assistance.

Sincerely,

Auditing Firm

Pre-Audit Questionnaire

Date:
Employer Name:

Please take a few moments to complete this questionnaire. When completed, it can be faxed to our office at ______________________ or e-mailed to: _________________________. Thank you for your cooperation.

Payroll System

1. Total number of employees on payroll

2. Total number of employees covered by the Collective Bargaining Agreement

3. Is the payroll prepared in-house or by an outside contractor? If outside contract, please name.

4. Has the same payroll system been in effect for the entire audit period?

5. Is the payroll organized into different departments? If so, what are the covered departments?

6. Are there any noncovered employees in the covered departments?

7. If there are no departments, how can covered employees be distinguished?

Reporting Procedures

1. When do contributions begin for new employees?
2. What types of hours are reported (regular, overtime, double-time)? Are all hours worked reported?
3. Do you limit the weekly contributions to 40 hours per week? If so, do you include overtime hours to reach the cap?
4. Are vacation hours reported? If so, when are they reported? When are they paid or taken?
5. Is accrued vacation paid to terminated employees reported to the Plan?
6. Are holiday hours reported?
7. Are any other paid nonworked hours reported on the contribution reports?

General

1. Has the same person prepared the contribution reports for the entire audit period?
2. If the preparer is not the contact person, is the contact person available to answer questions?
3. Has a temporary employment agency been used during the audit period? What kind of work did they perform for your company?
4. Did you issue any Form 1099s during the audit period? If so, to whom and for what?

Explanation of Employer's Accounting and Reporting System

Version 1

The employer began participation in the Plan on September 1, 2002.

The employer's payroll is divided into three departments. The names of these departments are Office, Yard, and Production. All contain covered employees. The department names are not necessarily indicative of the employees in them. Therefore, all departments were treated as one.

The employees punch timecards and the hours from timecards are put into a spreadsheet by Ms. L., who is located at the facility. Ms. L. then takes that spreadsheet and, from it, creates a new spreadsheet for the Plan, to use as a contribution report. She sends the original spreadsheet to the payroll manager at their main office, who then enters the hours into the AS400 payroll system.

Hire and term dates were not always accurate. The auditor verified them by looking up the employee's first and last check dates in the AS400 system.

There are several salaried employees who are covered by the CBA. These employees were reported for 160 hours during each month in which they worked the entire month, including months in which there were five weeks. The auditor picked up to 40 hours for each of these employees during five-week months.

Two employees received paychecks for 12 hours each after their term dates. These hours were not reported.

Other errors noted were considered clerical and were probably made by Ms. L. when she was manually entering hours into the Excel spreadsheet for the Plan.

Version 2

Prime Goods Factory, Inc.

During the audit period, two employees were responsible for the contribution reports. The current contact, Ms. X, has been responsible for the reporting since March 2004. Prior to March 2004, an employee named Ms. Y was in charge of the reports. However, responsibility for the holiday and vacation adjustments, which will be discussed later, changed monthly during the period prior to March 2004.

Electronic payroll records are kept in the Employer's Paypro system. The Employer switched to Paypro from its older mainframe system at the beginning of 2005. Records from August 2002 through the end of 2004 were transferred to the Paypro system. Older records are currently only available through the mainframe archives, which did not produce reliable reports.

A 100% population test of Q2 2002 showed that all employees who were covered by the production and maintenance collective bargaining agreement were reported. Firefighters and electricians are covered under separate CBAs, but are signatory to the same local union. Although the Fund agreement does not specifically exclude firefighters, the Auditor confirmed with the local union contact that the Fund agreement's intention was to exclude these job classes from contributions.

For the purposes of contribution reporting, the Employer prints a biweekly hours report from the payroll system. Parameters are set to exclude all holiday hours and some vacation hours. Parameters are set each time the report is run. They are not saved in the system. After the report is run, excluded vacation hours and holidays taken are added back onto the report using employee timecards. The adjustments are then entered into the system and, at the end of the month, a month-end report is run and printed to send to the Fund.

Note: Holidays worked are paid at the double-time rate and captured as both regular hours and holiday hours and, thus, they are excluded from the contribution reports. Floating holidays paid out to employees are also excluded from the contribution reports. Since all holiday hours are captured under the same earnings code, the Auditor used timecards and the Employer's Vacation Tracking System to verify that holiday types were reported correctly. It appears that they were.

It appears that the Employer failed to report hours paid to terminated employees during their final month of employment. For example, Mr. Z was terminated on April 12. He worked 72 hours from April 1-12 and was paid 80 hours of accrued vacation time upon termination. The Fund agreement stipulates that the Employer must report all vacation hours paid. Thus, the Employer should have reported 152 hours for Mr. Z during the month of April. However, his hours were omitted for the month of April because the Employer's month-end contribution report parameters capture only those employees who are active when the month-end report is run. Thus, the Auditor picked up all hours paid to terminated employees during the month of their termination.

The Employer failed to report call time and stand-by time, which are hours required by the CBA. The Employer never includes these hours when the contribution report is run. The Auditor picked up all call and stand-by time hours (earn codes 8 and 9, respectively) paid during the audit period.

The Auditor chose a larger than normal sample size in the new-hire test due to the Employer's description of some aspects of their reporting system—namely, that the Employer reports newly hired employees retroactively from 90 days after the date of hire. The Fund agreement requires that hours be reported retroactively from 60 days after the date of hire. Thus, the Auditor focused an expansion of normal testing for employees with tenure of between 60 and 90 days. Although one error was found in new-hire testing, it does not appear that the Employer has a systemic problem in reporting newly hired employees.

It appears that the Employer failed to report the week ending 9/01/20xx. The Employer failed to include the week in either September's or August's contribution report. This appears to be due to the manual nature of parameter setting in the running of contribution reports.

Vacation hours and other hours paid appear to be reported correctly.

Hire and Term Test

List employees to be tested, fill in hire, term dates where applicable.
Enter in the number of days in the probationary period in the space below.
Probationary period as per the CBA is _______ days.

Employee	SSN	Hire	Eligible	Reported	Date Term	Stop Reported
			01/00/00			
			01/00/00			
			01/00/00			
			01/00/00			
			01/00/00			
			01/00/00			
			01/00/00			
			01/00/00			
			01/00/00			
			01/00/00			
			01/00/00			
			01/00/00			
			01/00/00			
			01/00/00			
			01/00/00			
			01/00/00			
			01/00/00			
			01/00/00			
			01/00/00			
			01/00/00			

Once the number of days in the probationary period and the hire date are entered, the eligible date will be calculated.

Payroll Audit Report

ABC PLAN
Account Number 1234
Pertinent Information, Contract Terms and Deficiencies Determined

Schedule 1

PERTINENT INFORMATION

Employer Name and Address Company Name Address City, State, ZIP	Local Union Number 65 Date of Examination March 12, 2004
Employer Contact and Phone Number Mr. Employer Contact (555) 555-0000	Audit Period January 2001 through December 2003

SUMMARY OF CONTRACT TERMS

Contributions are due for each employee working in job classifications covered by the Collective Bargaining Agreement for each hour or portion thereof, which an employee works in such a job classification or receives pay in lieu of work (such as holiday, vacation, pro rata vacation, and severance pay) up to a maximum of 40 hours in any week for any one employee.

Effective Date	*Rate per Hour*
June 1, 2000	$1.85
June 1, 2001	$1.95
June 1, 2002	$2.15
June 1, 2003	$2.35

SUMMARY OF DEFICIENCIES $ 11,336.00

ABC PLAN
Account Number 1234
Payroll Audit Comments

Schedule 2

1. The purpose of the payroll audit is to determine the accuracy of the hours reported on the remittance reports and contributions paid by the Employer.
2. The Employer's payroll records are adequate for the reporting purposes and are well maintained. Remittance reports are prepared with reasonable care.
3. The Employer failed to report employees working in job classifications covered by the Collective Bargaining Agreement.
4. The Employer failed to report hours paid to new employees working in job classifications covered by the Collective Bargaining Agreement, from the first day of employment.
5. The Employer failed to report holiday hours paid to certain covered employees.

ABC PLAN
Account Number 1234
Summary of Errors in Employer's Contributions Reported to the Plan

Schedule 3

		2001	2002	2003	Total
E.	Failed to report employee in covered job classification.	—	$1,118.00	$9,080.00	$10,198.00
ED.	Failed to report new employee from date of hire.	—	206.40	419.60	626.00
H.	Failed to report holiday time.	—	103.20	408.80	512.00
		$ —	$1,427.60	$9,908.40	$11,336.00

ABC PLAN
Account Number 1234
Individual Summary of Misreported Hours for Audit Period

Schedule 4
Year: 2002

Primary Explanation of Deficiencies:
E. Failed to report employee in covered job classification.
ED. Failed to report new employee from date of hire.
H. Failed to report holiday time.

NAME	S/S NUMBER	NOTE	JAN	FEB	MAR	APR	MAY	JUNE	JULY	AUG	SEP	OCT	NOV	DEC	TOTAL
Davis, I	111-11-1111	E										160.00	160.00	200.00	520.00
Jones, E	777-77-7777	ED										72.00			72.00
Smith, John	888-88-8888	ED									24.00				24.00
Jones, E	777-77-7777	H											16.00	8.00	24.00
Smith, John	888-88-8888	H											16.00	8.00	24.00
		Total Hours	0.00	0.00	0.00	0.00	0.00	0.00	0.00	0.00	24.00	232.00	192.00	216.00	664.00
		Rate									$2.15	$2.15	$2.15	$2.15	
		Amount	$0.00	$0.00	$0.00	$0.00	$0.00	$0.00	$0.00	$0.00	$51.60	$498.80	$412.80	$464.40	$1,427.60

ABC PLAN
Account Number 1234
Individual Summary of Misreported Hours for Audit Period

Schedule 4
Year: 2003

Primary Explanation of Deficiencies:

E. Failed to report employee in covered job classification.
ED. Failed to report new employee from date of hire.
H. Failed to report holiday time.

NAME	S/S NUMBER	NOTE	JAN	FEB	MAR	APR	MAY	JUNE	JULY	AUG	SEP	OCT	NOV	DEC	TOTAL
Davis, I	111-11-1111	E		160.00	200.00	160.00	200.00	160.00	160.00	200.00	160.00	200.00	160.00	160.00	1,920.00
Doe, Jane	222-22-2222	E	160.00	160.00	200.00	160.00	200.00	160.00	160.00	200.00	160.00	200.00	160.00	160.00	2,080.00
Sample, J	333-33-3333	ED								120.00					120.00
Payne, April	444-44-4444	ED				64.00									64.00
Plot, James	555-55-5555	H					8.00		8.00		8.00		16.00	8.00	48.00
Sample, J	333-33-3333	H									8.00		16.00	8.00	32.00
Payne, April	444-44-4444	H					8.00		8.00		8.00		16.00	8.00	48.00
Winner, T	666-66-6666	H					8.00		8.00		8.00		16.00	8.00	48.00
		Total Hours	160.00	320.00	400.00	384.00	424.00	320.00	344.00	520.00	352.00	400.00	384.00	352.00	4,360.00
		Rate	$2.15	$2.15	$2.15	$2.15	$2.15	$2.35	$2.35	$2.35	$2.35	$2.35	$2.35	$2.35	
		Amount	$344.00	$688.00	$860.00	$825.60	$911.60	$752.00	$808.40	$1,222.00	$827.20	$940.00	$902.40	$827.20	$9,908.40

Questionnaire Regarding Double-Breasted Operations

	YES	NO	NOT KNOWN	WIP REF
1. Do the two entities share:				
a. Common officers?				
b. Common shareholders?				
c. Common management?				
2. Do the two entities use the same individuals for labor relations?				
3. Do the two entities share customers?				
4. Do the two entities conduct the same type of business?				
5. Do the two entities share the following services:				
a. Clerical?				
b. Accounting?				
c. Engineering?				
d. Estimating?				
6. Do the two entities have common insurance coverage?				
7. Do the two entities share equipment and/or supplies?				
8. Do the two entities share:				
a. Phone numbers?				
b. Bank accounts?				
c. Licenses?				
d. Tax returns?				
9. Do the two entities share:				
a. Current employees?				
b. Former employees?				
10. Do the two entities share:				
a. Offices?				
b. Shop?				
c. Equipment?				
d. Information technology equipment?				

Index